Addiction Recovery Through Buddhist Wisdom:

A Dharma Recovery Journal

Addiction Recovery Through Buddhist Wisdom:

A Dharma Recovery Journal

Steven L. Berg, PhD

Ehipassiko: Encouraging Investigation

2023

Copyright © 2023 Steven L. Berg

ISBN- 978-1-962024-02-0

In the spirit of Open Educational Resources (OERs)
and of not charging for the *dhamma*,
we have priced the paperback edition of
Addiction Recovery Through Buddhist Wisdom
at cost of production.

Neither the author nor publisher
receive royalties or other compensation for the sale of this book.
Free .pdf files of the book are available on our website.
http://ehipassikopress.org

Addiction Recovery Through Buddhist Wisdom
is licensed under a Creative Commons Attribution-NonCommercial-Share Alike 4.0 International License.

Please Note:

***Addiction Recovery Through Buddhist Wisdom*
is neither endorsed by nor affiliated with
Recovery Dharma Global.**

Dedicated to

**Nicholas Andrew Jetton
(1994 - 2023)**

Table of Contents

"Acknowledgements" v

Introduction 1

Inquiry Questions 7

Chapter 1: The First Noble Truth 11

Chapter 2: The Second Noble Truth 19

Chapter 3: The Third Noble Truth 27

Chapter 4: The Fourth Noble Truth 33

Chapter 5: Wise Understanding 39

Chapter 6: Wise Intention 45

Chapter 7: Making Amends 51

Chapter 8: Wise Speech 59

Chapter 9: Wise Action 67

Chapter 10: The First Precept 71

Chapter 11: The Second Precept 75

Chapter 12: The Third Precept 79

Chapter 13: The Fourth Precept 85

Chapter 14: The Fifth Precept 91

Chapter 15: Wise Livelihood 97

Chapter 16: Wise Effort 105

Chapter 17: Wise Mindfulness 111

Chapter 18: Wise Concentration 119

Appendix: Reflections on Art, Buddhism, and Recovery 127

    Cover 129

    Frontispiece 131

    Acknowledgements 133

    Introduction 135

    Dedication 137

    Table of Contents 139

    Inquiry Questions 141

    The First Noble Truth 143

    The Second Noble Truth 145

    The Third Noble Truth 147

    The Fourth Noble Truth 149

    Wise Understanding 151

    Wise Intention 153

    Making Amends 155

    Wise Speech 157

    Wise Action 159

    The First Precept 161

    The Second Precept 163

    The Third Precept 165

    The Fourth Precept 167

    The Fifth Precept 169

"Acknowledgements" vii

Wise Livelihood 171

Wise Effort 173

Wise Mindfulness 175

Wise Concentration 177

Appendix 179

Acknowledgments

This book would not have been possible without the support of Cathy N. Davidson. Cathy was instrumental in arranging for HASTAC to publish my *Promoting Student Transformation at the Community College* (2020) and in having the City University of New York release it on their website as an Open Educational Resource. Cathy also encouraged me to illustrate the book. She then worked with me as we brought out the paperback edition, an edition sold at cost of production where neither I nor my publisher received royalties or any other compensation. Cathy was not directly involved with the development of *Addiction Recovery Through Buddhist Wisdom*, but had I not had the experience of working with her on the previous book, this book would not have been possible.

When Steven Fischer saw a journal that combined *Recovery Dharma's* "Inquiry Questions" and my art that I had made as a gift for someone, his immediate response was "You must publish this." He has followed the progress of the book and provided insightful advice since the beginning.

There are three people at Schoolcraft College who have been particularly supportive over the years tolerating me as I geeked out over my research, listening to me discuss my latest projects, and becoming dear personal friends as well as valued professional colleagues: Josselyn Moore, Jessica Worden-Jones, and Kim Lark.

I remember the first time I met Bhante Muditha. He and Bhanthe Sankichcha have been my two primary teachers on how to follow the Buddha *dhamma*. I am also grateful for the support I have received from the devotees who attend the Great Lakes Buddhist Vihara, my spiritual home.

I am grateful to Recovery Dharma Global for allowing me to reprint the questions from the second edition of *Recovery Dharma* in this book.

Finally, there are the group of people who called themselves The Back Porch Group.

Introduction

When I stopped drinking on 23 March 1983, there were no recovery programs organized around the Buddha *dhamma*. I would have more than twenty years of sobriety before I took the Five Precepts for the first time and began to live as a Buddhist in the Theravada tradition. I did not read *Recovery Dharma* whose "Inquiry Questions" are incorporated into this book, until I had been sober for almost 40 years.

My early research as an academic revolved around recovery. I wrote my dissertation on *AA, Spiritual Issues, and the Treatment of Lesbian and Gay Alcoholics*[1] (1989). I edited *Alcoholism and Pastoral Ministry* (1989) and wrote three annotated bibliographs concerning lesbian and gay alcoholics/addicts (1987), Jewish alcoholics/addicts (1993), and spirituality and addiction (1993). My articles promoting recovery appeared in popular publications, pornographic magazines, and a journal that required its content to be consistent with the official teachings of the magisterium of the Catholic Church. But I did not investigate how Buddhism could be used for addiction recovery.

The first book I became aware of on the relationship between recovery and Buddhism was Kevin Griffin's *One Breath at a Time: Buddhism and the Twelve Steps* (2004) which was published after I had stopped focusing my research on addiction, recovery, and God talk in AA.

I was introduced to *Recovery Dharma* when my nephew, Nick Jetton, asked me to purchase a copy of the book for him. When I ordered Nick's copy, I bought a copy for myself. Unlike my nephew, I had long experience in both sobriety and as a practicing Buddhist. I wondered how I might have reacted to the book had I read it in 1983 when I knew nothing about recovery or Buddhism?

My current academic research focuses on the Brahma Viharas which are the four states of mind that allow us to cultivate positive behaviors while eliminating those behaviors that are harmful. They are compassion, loving kindness, equanimity, and sympathetic joy. As an academic, I am especially interested in the role of compassion in education. Although not specifically mentioned, the relationship between the Brahma Viharas and education was a focus of my *Promoting Student Transformation at the Community College* (2020). Yet the point remains that, although I am a sober Buddhist, I have no experience using the *dhamma* to recover from addiction. I had already recovered before being introduced to *dhamma*.

---

[1] My early work with LGBTQ+ issues and recovery was a product of the socio-cultural period in which it was produced, a culture where the word "queer" was still a pejorative term.

Relationship Between *Recovery Dharma* and *Addiction Recovery Through Buddhist Wisdom*

Recovery Dharma Global is an international organization founded in 2019 to offer a recovery program based on Buddhist principles. They published the book *Recovery Dharma* that serves as a guide to their program, a book that includes a series of "Questions for Inquiry." Because *Recovery Dharma* was published under a Creative Commons Attribution-ShareAlike 4.0 International License, I can legally and ethically include their questions in this book.

Even though *Addiction Recovery Through Buddhist Practice* includes the questions from *Recovery Dharma*, it is neither affiliated with nor endorsed by Recovery Dharma Global.

Genesis of *Addiction Recovery Through Buddhist Wisdom*

A young man in early recovery told me that he was interested in journaling but preferred to have prompts. He also told me that he had an interest in Buddhism and liked the approach that *Recovery Dharma* took.

I printed out the "Inquiry Questions" and pasted one on each page of a journal I purchased for him. I created a portrait of this man and placed it in the front of the journal and then pasted other pieces of my *dhamma* inspired art at the beginning of each section. When I showed the completed gift to Dr. Steven Fischer, his immediate response was that I should publish it.

Rather than simply reproducing the questions from *Recovery Dharma* with old images, I created all new art for this book. I then wrote short reflections inspired by the art and the Buddhist principles they represent. My reflections take an interdisciplinary approach to how I live the Buddha *dhamma* in my sober life.

A Note on Buddhist Terminology

Except for the subtitle for *Addiction Recovery Through Buddhist Wisdom: A Dharma Recovery Journal* and for references to Recovery Dharma Global and their book, I use Theravada Buddhist terms which are written in Pali instead of the more common Mahayana terms written in Sanskrit. These include *dhamma* instead of *dharma* and *suttas* instead of *sutras*. However, I mostly avoid Pali terms except for references to the *dhamma*.

Eclectic Sources

In his introduction to *The Noble Eightfold Path*, Bhikkhu Bodhi provides a cautionary warning that, on its surface strikes fear into eclectic artists like me who pull material from a variety of sources. He is rightly concerned about those individuals who may "combine Buddhist mindfulness meditation with sessions of Hindu mantra recitation, Christian prayer with Sufi dancing, Jewish Kabbala with Tibetan visualization exercises."

Such picking and choosing, according to Bodhi, is problematic for two reasons. First, such an approach compromises the traditions from which it draws. Second, spiritual practices are built on a vision of reality and the visions from these various traditions are not mutually compatible. Yet, in my art—as well as in my personal and academic lives—I benefit from an extremely eclectic approach.

While I consult a variety of sources, I avoid the problems Bodhi identifies because I am clear that I follow the Buddhist path toward enlightenment. Sometimes I do it well. At other times not so well. But I am unquestionably a Buddhist and this is a Buddhist inspired book. But this does not mean that non-Buddhists cannot benefit from it.

Learning about other traditions can help me better understand my practice. For example, reading the story of the Last Judgement where Jesus tells his followers that "whatever you do for even the least of your brothers and sisters, that you do unto me" might help me better understand the message of the *Karaniya Metta Sutta* which focuses on loving kindness. Yet, I do not create a mishmash of colliding worldviews into a single practice for myself. I remain a Buddhist who has a richer appreciation for the Buddha *dhamma* because I have studied Christian and other scriptures, philosophies, and approaches to life.

In recovery, I believe that it is also necessary to have a primary focus. Answering *Recovery Dharma's* "Inquiry Questions" is similar to taking a fourth step in Alcoholics Anonymous, but they are different activities inspired by different paths inspired by different worldviews. An AA alcoholic would benefit from answering *Recovery Dharma's* questions found in this journal as well as in reading my reflections found in the Appendix. Individuals in Recovery Dharma can benefit from considering the fourth step questions found in *Alcoholics Anonymous*, more commonly known as the Big Book. There are individuals from other recovery programs or who suffer from addictions other than alcohol/drugs who would also benefit from this book.

Placement of Reflections

When this book was in its infancy, someone whom I highly respect suggested that the reflections ought to immediately follow the art at the beginning of each chapter. "If they are at the back," he argued, "people might not read them." I replied, "That is the point."

Addiction Recovery Through Buddhist Wisdom is primarily designed as a journal that makes it easy for people to reflect on their own experiences. The Buddhist inspired art is meant to be enjoyed, not necessarily analyzed. And my reflections are not meant as a guide on how you should reflect on the prompts found on each page. In fact, it is better for you to read *Recovery Dharma* to get such guidance than it is for you to read my reflections. This book is laid out in the same order as *Recovery Dharma* to make it easier to do so.

When—and if—you read my reflections, my desire is that they serve as additional prompts for you to consider the role of the Buddha *dhamma* in your own life and how it contributes to your sobriety. The reflections are part of a wider conversation you are having with yourself, trusted friends, recovery literature, the *suttas* and other Buddhist commentaries such as Bhikku Bodi's *The Noble Eightfold Path*, materials from other worldviews, and so forth.

A Note on Royalties

In the spirit of Open Educational Resources and the tradition of not selling the *dhamma*, *Addiction Recovery Through Buddhist Wisdom* was published by Ehipassiko Press, LLC and is sold at the cost of production. Free versions of the book are available at the Ehipassiko Press website. Neither I nor Ehipassiko Press receive royalties or any other compensation from the distribution of this book.

Steven L. Berg, PhD
Professor of English and History
Schoolcraft College
October 2023

"Inquiry Questions"

According to the book *Recovery Dharma* from which they have been reprinted, "These Inquiry Questions are intended to be a useful tool for supporting our growth and recovery. They can be used as part of a formal process of self-investigation or inventory with a mentor, wise friend, or group; as tools to explore a specific life situation; as guides for a daily self-inquiry practice; as meeting discussion topics; or any other way you may find helpful on your path of awakening and freedom from addiction and habitual behavior."

Why Reprint These "Inquiry Questions" in a Separate Book?

Recovery Dharma provides excellent "Inquiry Questions" at the end of each section. However, because the book was not designed as a journal, there is inadequate space to answer the questions where they appear. This book was designed to provide the space necessary to reflect on the "Inquiry Questions."

Saying that *Recovery Dharma* was not designed as a journal is not a criticism of the book. In fact, you will get more out of this book if you read *Recovery Dharma* while completing the prompts.[2]

Although I break the content into more chapters than does *Recovery Dharma*, the organization of the two books is identical. You can read the sections in *Recovery Dharma* and then easily respond to the prompts in this book.

Although the prompts were published in *Recovery Dharma*, this book is not affiliated with Recovery Dharma Global. The thoughts in the reflections as well as the art are mine and are neither endorsed by Recovery Dharma Global nor represent positions taken by that organization.

I hope that this book facilitates your reflection as you grow in the Buddha *dhamma* and in your recovery. Neither I nor Ehipassiko Press receive royalties or other compensation for distribution of *Addiction Recovery Through Buddhist Wisdom*. Free versions of the book are available on the Ehipassiko Press website. The paperback edition is sold at the cost of production.

---

[2] This book uses the "Inquiry Questions" published in the second edition of *Recovery Dharma* (July 2023) which have been revised from the first edition. However, the order for both editions is the same. Therefore, *Addiction Recovery Through Buddhist Wisdom* is compatible with either edition of *Dharma Recovery*.

Chapter 1:

The First Noble Truth

The truth of dukkha / pervasive dissatisfaction.

Begin by making a list of the behaviors and actions associated with your addiction(s) that you consider harmful. Without exaggerating or minimizing, think about the things you have done that have created additional suffering to yourself and others.

For each behavior listed, write how you have suffered because of that behavior, and write how others have suffered because of that behavior. List any other costs or negative consequences you can think of, such as finances, health, relationships, sexual relations, or missed opportunities.

Do you notice any patterns? What are they? What are the ways that you might avoid or reduce suffering for yourself and others if you change these patterns?

How have your addictive behaviors been a response to trauma and pain? What are some ways you can respond to trauma and pain that nurture healing rather than avoidance?

If you have experienced trauma from discrimination, what are ways you can experience healing and practice self-care? Consider opportunities to support social justice while allowing yourself to heal and practice compassion for yourself and others.

Chapter 2:

The Second Noble Truth

The truth of the causes of dukkha / pervasive dissatisfaction.

"The Second Noble Truth" 21

List situations, circumstances, and feelings that you have used harmful behavior to try to avoid.

Name the emotions, sensations, and thoughts that come to mind when you abstain. Are there troubling memories, shame, grief, or unmet needs behind the craving? How can you meet these with compassion and patience?

What things did you give up in your clinging to impermanent and unreliable solutions? For example, did you give up relationships, financial security, health, opportunities, legal standing, or other important things to maintain your addictive behaviors? What made the addiction more important to you than any of these things you gave up?

Are you clinging to any beliefs that fuel craving and aversion, beliefs that deny the truth of impermanence, or beliefs about how things in life "should" be? What are they?

If you have experienced discrimination-based trauma or social injustice, how can you meet the experience in a way that honors your true self, without creating more pain and suffering?

Chapter 3:

The Third Noble Truth

The truth of the end of dukkha / pervasive dissatisfaction.

What makes it so hard to quit?

What resources are available to help you abstain and recover?

List reasons to believe you can recover. Also list your doubts. What might the wise and compassionate part of you — your Buddha nature — say about these doubts?

Practice "letting go" of something small. Notice that the craving doesn't last and that there's a little sense of relief when you let it pass. That's a little taste of freedom.

Chapter 4:

The Fourth Noble Truth

The truth of the path that leads to the end of suffering which is known as the Eightfold Path.

"The Fourth Noble Truth" 35

Understanding that recovery and the ending of suffering is possible, what is your path to recovery and ending the suffering of addiction? Be honest about the challenges you might face, and the tools and resources you will use to meet those challenges.

What behavior can you change to more fully support your recovery?

What does it mean to you to take refuge in the Buddha, the Dharma, and the Sangha for your recovery?

Chapter 5:

Wise Understanding

Think of a situation in your life that is causing confusion or unease:

1. What is the truth of this situation?
2. Are you seeing clearly, or are you getting lost in judgment, taking things personally in stories you're telling yourself, or repeating past messages you've internalized? How?
3. Is your vision clouded by greed, hatred, confusion, clinging, attachment, or craving? How?

In what situations and parts of your life do you have the most difficulty separating wants from needs? Are there areas or relationships where the drive to get what you desire overshadows any other consideration? Has this changed since you began or continue in recovery?

Are there parts of your life where you are driven to continue unpleasant experiences because you think you "must" or "need to?"

How is karma — the law of cause and effect — showing up right now? Where in your life are you dealing with the effects or aftermath of action you took in the past, both positive and negative?

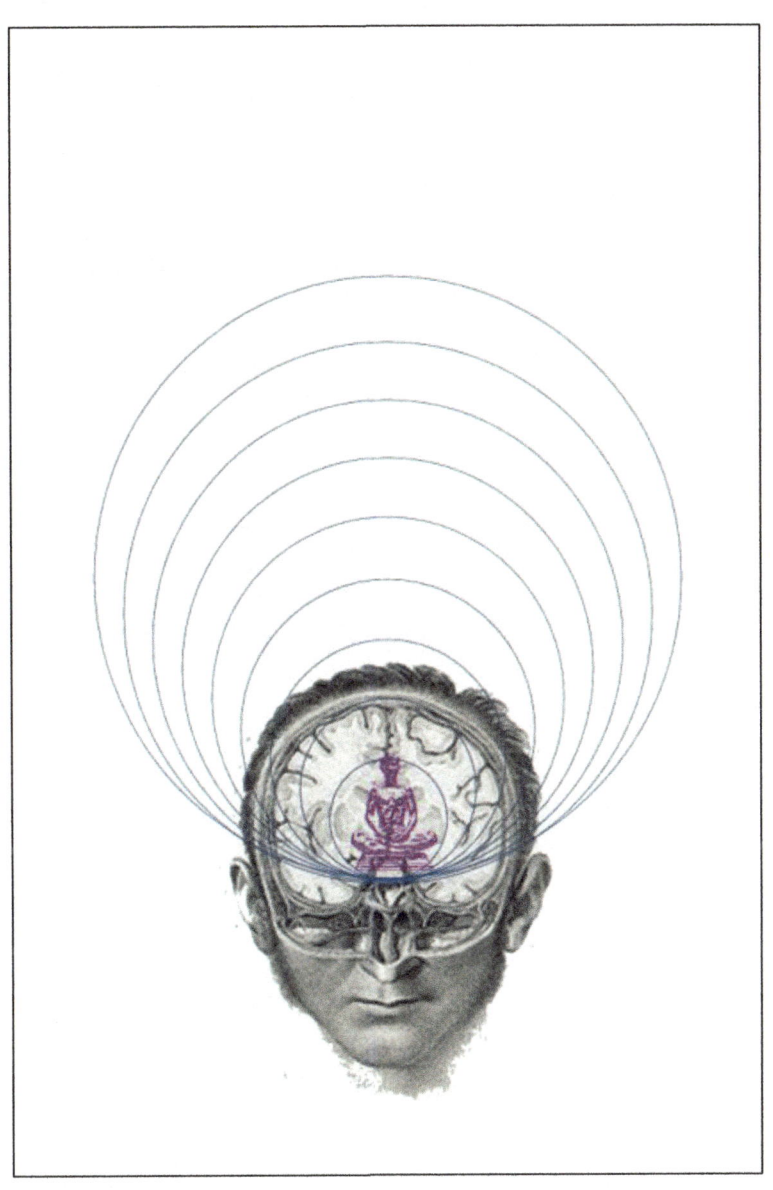

Chapter 6:

Wise Intention

What compassion or forgiveness can you offer when someone's intention is good but their impact is harmful? If it doesn't feel safe or appropriate to offer this directly to the person, how can you bring that forgiveness into your own heart so you don't have the burden of carrying it?

During your periods of addictive behavior, how did you act in ways that were clinging, uncaring, harsh, cruel, or unforgiving? Toward whom (including yourself) were these feelings directed? How might generosity, compassion, lovingkindness, and forgiveness have changed your behavior?

What actions have you taken that have harmed others? Have you formed an intention to reconcile with both yourself and the person or people you've harmed (to make amends)? If so, have you found a wise friend or mentor you can go to for guidance and support in the amends process, (which is summarized below)? What support can this person provide as you begin the process of amends?

Chapter 7:

Making Amends

"Making Amends" 53

Have you done something intentionally that you now recognize caused harm to another? Who has been harmed by your actions?

Have you honestly formed the intention not to repeat harmful actions and to learn from the experience in future interactions? Have you begun the process of directly addressing the harmful actions of your past?

Making amends depends on the circumstance, including your present relationship to the person and the extent to which you can undo the harm caused through direct actions (like correcting a public dishonesty or compensating another for things you have taken that were not freely offered). Ask yourself, "What can I do in the present?"

Can you address and reconcile with the harm you have caused without forming an attachment to being forgiven? Identify the motivation for making each amends.

What actions would restore balance in your own feelings and approach to whatever harm you have caused? Can these steps be taken without causing new harm to the person or the relationship?

If you're experiencing a difficult situation or choice in your life right now, investigate the intention you are bringing to this situation.

1. Are you being selfish or self-seeking? How?
2. Are you being driven by aversion (running away from an unpleasant experience) or craving (grasping for pleasure)? How?
3. How could you bring in a spirit of generosity, compassion, lovingkindness, appreciative joy, and forgiveness to this situation?
4. How would this situation look different if you brought these factors to mind before reacting or responding?
5. If you don't want to, can you at least have the intention and willingness to do so?

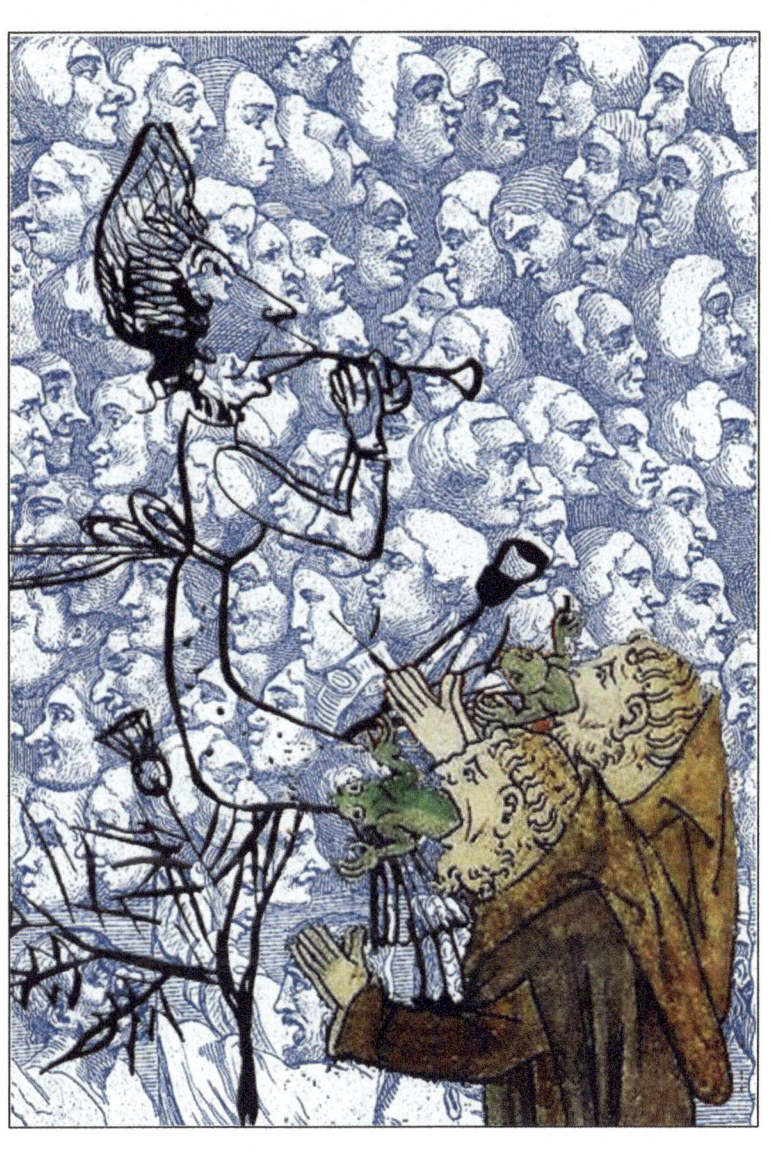

Chapter 8:

Wise Speech

Have you caused harm with your speech? How?

Have you been dishonest or harsh in your communication? When, and in what specific ways?

Do you use speech now to hurt or control people, to present a false idea or image of yourself or of reality, to demand attention, or to relieve the discomfort of silence? Detail specific instances in which you used speech to mislead, misdirect, or distract.

Are you careful to avoid causing harm with your speech?

Do you say things you know are not true, or pretend to know the truth about something when you don't, to appear more knowledgeable or credible than you are? List some examples.

Chapter 9:

Wise Action

Have you acted in a way that was unskillful or that created suffering? How?

During those times you were unskillful or created suffering, how would it have changed the outcome if you had acted out of compassion, kindness, generosity, and forgiveness? Would you now have a different emotional or mental response to your past actions if you had acted with these principles in mind?

Chapter 10:

The First Precept

To refrain from taking life.

"The First Precept" 73

Have you caused harm? How? Allow for a broad understanding of harm, including physical, emotional, mental, and karmic harm such as financial, legal, moral, microaggression, or any of the "isms" and phobias such as racism, sexism, ableism, classism, homophobia, transphobia, etc.

Even if you can't point to specific harms that you have caused, have you acted in a way that purposely avoided being aware of the possibility of harm?

Chapter 11:

The Second Precept

To refrain from taking what is not freely given.

People "take" in many ways: we take goods or material possessions, we take time and energy, we take care and recognition. With this broad understanding of taking, have you taken what has not been freely given? How? What are specific examples or patterns where this has been true for you?

Chapter 12:

The Third Precept

To refrain from sensuous misconduct.

"The Third Precept" 81

Have you behaved irresponsibly, selfishly, or without full consent and awareness (from yourself or partners) in your sexual conduct? How?

Reviewing your sexual partners or activities, have you been fully aware in each instance of other existing relationships, prior or current mental or emotional conditions of yourself and your partner(s), and your own intentions in becoming sexually involved? How or how not?

Has your sexual activity, both by yourself and with others, been based on non-harmful intentions? Have you entered into each sexual activity with awareness and understanding? How or how not?

Chapter 13:

The Fourth Precept

To refrain from false speech.

"The Fourth Precept" 87

Have you been dishonest? How?

What patterns did your dishonesty take? Did you act or speak dishonestly to deny or misrepresent the truth about your own behavior or status?

Were there particular situations in which your dishonesty was particularly present (for instance: when dealing with your addictive behaviors, in job or professional settings, among friends, with family)? Investigate the source of the dishonesty in each setting: Was it based on greed, confusion, fear, denial? Why were you lying?

Chapter 14:

The Fifth Precept

*To refrain from alcohol
and other intoxicants that cloud the mind.*

Have you used intoxicants or other behaviors that cloud your ability to see clearly?

What substances and behaviors have you become reliant on to change or cloud your awareness? Has this changed over time? Or, if you have periods of abstinence, were your habitual intoxicants or behaviors replaced by other ways to avoid awareness of your present circumstances and conditions? How?

List ways you might practice the Five Precepts, compassion, lovingkindness, and generosity in your decision-making.

Chapter 15:

Wise Livelihood

Does your job cause harm? What is the specific nature of that harm?

How can you do your job more mindfully and with an intention of compassion and non-harm?

Do you bring an understanding of karma and kindness to your job, or do you compartmentalize it and exclude it from awareness of wise action?

What part does greed play in the choices you make in your livelihood? Does greed get in the way of awareness or compassion?

How can you be of service in your community?

How might you bring a spirit of generosity to your life, both in your profession and outside it?

Chapter 16:

Wise Effort

What efforts have you made to connect with a wise friend, mentor, or dharma buddy who can help you develop and balance your efforts?

Think of a situation that is causing you discomfort or unease. What is the nature of the effort you're bringing to the situation? Pay attention to whether it feels balanced and sustainable, or if you're leaning too far in the direction of either inactivity or overexertion?

Are you dealing with overwhelming desires, aversions, laziness or discouragement, restlessness and worry, or doubt about your own ability to recover? How do these hindrances affect the choices you're making?

Are you avoiding feelings by checking out and giving up, or through obsessive busyness and perfectionism?

Chapter 17:

Wise Mindfulness

What are steps you can take to support a regular meditation practice?

What are steps you can take to practice mindfulness throughout the day by checking in with yourself about how you're feeling, and pausing before reacting to situations?

What are steps you can take to sit with your discomfort instead of running from it or running toward temporary pleasure?

What are steps you can take to question the "truths" that your mind tells you, rather than automatically believing them? Identify specific instances where your mind and perceptions "lied" to you about the truth of a situation, and how being aware of that might have changed your reaction and led to a less harmful outcome.

Think about times when you felt fear, doubt, or hesitation. Now, let yourself become aware of their temporary nature. How might that awareness have led to an outcome that was less harmful?

Chapter 18:

Wise Concentration

How do you get unfocused or distracted in meditation?

What are steps you can take to refocus your mind without judging your own practice?

Notice what value or learning you could gain by carefully and kindly noticing where your mind has gone, or what has distracted you.

What are steps you can take to use concentration to see clearly and act wisely?

What are steps you can take to be kind and gentle with yourself through this process?

Appendix:

Reflections on Art, Buddhism, and Recovery

"Appendix: Reflections on Art, Buddhism, and Recovery" 129

Cover

The cover of a book signals what we can expect when we open the book and view the pages it contains. Sometimes, we start by considering the title, *Addiction Recovery Through Buddhist Wisdom: A Dharma Recovery Journal*.

- **Addiction Recovery**: The book is about recovery from addiction. Although you will later learn that the primary focus is recovery from addiction to alcohol and other drugs, it can be a useful tool for people recovering from other addictions as well.

- **Through**: It is written from a particular perspective or worldview.

- **Buddhist Wisdom**: That worldview is Buddhism. However, although the primary perspective is Buddhism, people from other spiritual, religious, or philosophical traditions—or from no tradition at all—can also benefit by using the book as a tool to reflect on their own addiction recovery.

- **A Dharma Recovery Journal**: The book includes space for the reader to write and to reflect in it. It can be used as a journal.

Sometimes we focus on the images on the book cover even before we read the title. What do those images suggest to you?

How are they inviting? What about them signals that this book is welcoming?

Once we identify as people who live sober lives through the Buddha *dhamma*, we begin to serve as the cover for both recovery and the *dhamma*. After seeing how we live our lives, others will judge sober living and Buddhism by our example. This is especially true if we identify with a specific organization, recovery meeting, Buddhist sect, or temple. Are we inviting or not? Do we exhibit Right Actions that reflect well on those organizations?

Although I am not a member of Recovery Dharma and have never attended a Recovery Dharma meeting, I am mindful that, as the author of this book, people will assume I am associated with it. I conduct myself accordingly.

Because I have been associated with the Great Lakes Buddhist Vihara for more than 17 years, people will associate my Buddhist practice with that specific temple. Do I represent the temple well? Do I greet new people with the same openness that I was welcomed into the community when I first arrived? Do I take the time to explain to a newcomer where to put their shoes, where they can find the restrooms, and other expectations to make them feel more comfortable. Do I make sure that they are included in conversations and have access to the types of literature that they desire? Am I a cover that makes them want to open the book of the Buddha *dhamma*? Do my actions make it desirable for them to return.

If you are a member of Recovery Dharma or Alcoholics Anonymous or some other recovery program, do you welcome the new person and do similar things as I do at temple? Do your Wise Actions demonstrate that you have the type of sobriety that they might want to emulate?

The book's cover makes a promise, I hope that the contents live up to your expectations of it.

Elements in *Cover*

The art on the cover includes Eizan Kikukawa's woman writing (c. 1804-1810), the tintype *Discarded Vices* (c. 1860-1880), and an image of the Gautama Buddha. "Plate II: Lotus. Japanese Name Hasu" was created by Kazumasa Ogawa and was published in his *Some Japanese Flowers* (c. 1895).

Frontispiece

A book's frontispiece originally included architectural elements such as columns that were used to decorate the title page. During the seventeenth century, the frontispiece moved to the page opposite the title page and would often include a portrait of the author while providing readers with insight into the book's content.

Because of the Buddhist doctrine of *anatman* or no-self, it might seem a curious choice to include Socrates' directive to "Know Thyself" in the frontispiece of this book. How can I know myself if there is no self?

Early recovery is not a time to employ theological language as part of philosophical or doctrinal debates on the nature of *anatman*. Instead, it is a time for us to use common language to understand our actual relationship to the world. We journal so that we can know ourselves better because it is only by knowing our current selves that we can begin to make the changes in our lives that support long term recovery.

Although I could have included my image in the frontispiece as the "author" of this book, ultimately *Addiction Recovery Through Buddhist Wisdom* is not my book. It is a book that you will write as you reflect on the questions developed by Recovery Dharma.

The human image I did include made me think of the *Satipatthana Sutta* which, in part, reminds us that our body is a manifold of impurity for which we should have no attachment. This Christian image suggests the very Buddhist idea that part of knowing ourselves is realizing that we are mortal and are subject to the cycle of life, death, and rebirth.

The background image is of Mahakala who, in Tantric Buddhism is a destroyer of obstacles to Enlightenment. As part of knowing ourselves, we learn who in our lives will help us on our path toward recovery. Who are the wise friends and mentors who will walk the path with us? Some might be in recovery programs. Some might be therapists or other medical professionals. Some might be supportive family or friends.

In Buddhism, the community is one of the three parts of the triple gem in which we take refuge: the Buddha (example), the *dhamma* (teaching), and the *sangha* (community). We do not grow spiritually on our own. Nor do we, by ourselves, gain contented sobriety. We flourish as part of a community.

When we enter recovery, we can see that our lives have been filled with mud. But as Thich Nhat Hanh argues in *No Mud, No Lotus*, without the mud of pervasive dissatisfaction, there can be no lotus of happiness. The idea that nothing in our past can prevent us from blossoming in the future is related to the inspirational story of Aṅgulimāla. Prior to meeting the Gautama Buddha, Aṅgulimāla wore a neckless of 999 fingers, one from each person he had killed. Instead of adding one of the Buddha's fingers to his neckless, Aṅgulimāla became a disciple of the Buddha and obtained enlightenment.

Regardless of the mud in our lives, I doubt that anyone completing this journal will have covered themselves with the mud of a serial killer who has murdered 999 people. If there is hope for Aṅgulimāla, there is hope for us.

Elements in *Frontispiece*

This piece includes a mosaic from the first century. It was excavated from the convent of San Gregorio, Via Appia in Rome, Italy. It combines the Greek motto *gnōthi sauton* (know thyself) with a skeleton who communicates the warning *Respice post te; hominem te esse memento; memento mori* (Look behind; remember that you are mortal; remember death.) The background is an image of Mahakala who, in Tantric Buddhism destroys obstacles to enlightenment (c. 1400s). Mahakala, is also found in Hinduism where he is a manifestation of Shiva. The image was created in Western Tibet, possibly at the Tholing Monastery. The final element in this piece is a hand colored photograph of a lotus created by Ogawa Kazumasa in 1896.

Acknowledgements

As a graduate student, I studied the myth of the American Adam, the rugged individual who depends only on themself. The American Adam is exemplified in Benjamin Franklin's self-made man and in the stories of Davey Crocket and the women in his life. We see it in the expressive poetry written by Walt Whitman and in Henry David Thoreau's essay on "Self Reliance." Although such individualism is part of the fabric of American culture, none of us—not even Franklin nor Crocket nor Whitman nor Thoreau—can survive as an individual.

While spending time growing beans next to his cabin on Walden Pond where he wrote about self reliance, Thoreau's mother was doing his laundry. And it is easy to be proud that your bean crop will make you self reliant when you can answer the Emerson's dinner bell whenever you desire. Thoreau was not self reliant. We all depend on community.

Charles Darwin's work is often described as "survival of the fittest," a characterization that is a misrepresentation of his main thesis. Darwin actually argues that species can only survive by showing each other sympathy, a nineteenth century term that today could be translated as "compassion."

When I first saw the photograph of Frank M. Howe and Velorus W. Bruce supporting each other, I was taken by the powerful statement these two veterans were making. Arguably, each could have had a crutch or some other non-human devise to hold themselves up. Yet they knew that we can only survive and flourish in community, that, if we are divided, we will fall.

This book and every other project in my life is the result of a community that can often be traced back for years or even generations. People who died before I was born influenced the people who have become part of my spiritual, recovery, academic, and personal *sangha*/community.

As a sober person who follows the Buddha *dhamma*, it is important that I acknowledge the contributions of those who support me. Sometimes I can do this directly by picking up the tab for Saturday morning coffee some friends and I enjoy at Café Even after our morning meditation class. Or I might purchase a book for a friend.

Saying "thank you" to the members of our communities is important, but it is not enough. I must act with the same generosity which others have shown me. For example, I continue to share the generosity given to me by professors such as Cathy N. Davidson, Mary Lee Schneider, George Landon, and others with how I treat my students today.

Expressing gratitude is not a zero-sum game where there is only so much gratitude to go around. Anne Sexton ends her poem "What the Bird with the Human Head Knew" with the insight, "Abundance is scooped from abundance, yet abundance remains." Generosity and gratitude are not depleted by sharing them. So share we must.

Elements in *Acknowledgements*

The focal point is a portrait of Civil War veterans Frank M. Howe and Velorus W. Bruce. Behind the men is a detail from Umberto Boccioni's *Dynamism of a Man's Head* (1913). The foreground is Maurice Denis' *April* (1892) and the background is Gustav Klimt's *Bauerngarten* (1907). A biological sketch of a raspberry created by the Department of Agriculture is found in the foreground (1891).

Introduction

Even though not a single reflection had been written and the only art that had been created for *Addiction Recovery Through Buddhist Wisdom* was the "Frontispiece," the first thing I wrote in this book was the "Introduction." Writing the "Introduction" before the rest of the book offered me a road map that provided a clear vision of what I hoped to accomplish. I knew that what I initially wrote would change, but I needed a plan.

The Noble Eightfold Path gives us a roadmap to follow as we move along our path to recovery. Although the path doesn't change, our understanding of how to incorporate the Noble Truths into our lives does change over time. Our overall path remains consistent but, as time passes, we see details differently.

When I started down the Noble Eightfold Path, I didn't even realize that such a path existed. I know someone must have mentioned it to me or that I had come across it while doing academic research, but the Noble Eightfold Path was only a tangential part of my spiritual program. I focused on the Five Precepts: refraining from killing, refraining from stealing, refraining from sensuous misconduct, refraining from lying, and refraining from intoxicants. But the path was there guiding me, nonetheless. Because I had over 20 years of uninterrupted sobriety before I began following the Buddha *dhamma*, I never used Buddhism as the basis for my recovery. Yet, my experience shows that Buddhism works as a tool to advance contented sobriety.

The Fifth Precept directs us to refrain from mind altering substances, but that is not our entire path. To simply stop drinking is not the same as recovering from alcoholism or other drug addictions. The white-knuckle sobriety I experienced when I first stopped drinking is something I could not have maintained—nor would have wanted to maintain—for the rest of my life.

I first had to stop drinking to learn the tools provided by the roadmap that initially gave me my introduction to contented sobriety. Fortunately, that roadmap, like the Eightfold path, came with directions which lead to a quality life.

Elements in *Introduction*

The main image is Vilhelm Hammershøi's *Interior with Young Man Reading* (1889). The wall behind him is Charles Rennie Mackintosh's *Butterfly Flower, Bowling* (1912). Bowling is a small village near Glasgow. In one of the picture frames, I placed an image of Krampus in a bottle which was originally published as a postcard. Krampus is a demon/goat figure from Central European folklore. Schnapps was the traditional drink to offer Krampus. The other picture frame holds an image of the Gautama Buddha.

Dedicated To Nick Jetton

Because I am both a professor of history as well as a genealogist, in 2014, I was asked by the editor of *The International Agenda* to review Andrea Stuart's *Sugar in the Blood* in which she traces the legacy of her eighth great-grandfather, George Ashby (c. 1620-1676). Stuart argued that we are made by the places we love. Although this finding is valid for Stuart and her family, I am not sure that it applies to the Liberacki-Wilcox lineage that Nick Jetton and I share. My experience is that we are shaped by the people we love and who love us.

As genealogists, Stuart and I have it easy because we are tracing individuals from the past to the present. It is much more difficult to speculate on the legacy of our contemporaries. It is even harder to consider what our own legacies might be. Generally, there is no clear way for us to measure where our influence travels.

A couple years ago, I arrived at my office to find a package against the door. On the outside was written: "To Dr. Berg. From [a name I didn't recognize]." Inside the package was a beautiful piece of original art the person had created for me.

I confirmed that this individual was a former student from about five years previous. From my records, I could not identify anything special I had ever done for this student. But I obviously had had an impact on their life. Their gift still hangs in my office as a reminder that we cannot know the legacy—for good or evil—of the individual actions we take.

During my life, there have been many individuals who have influenced me, individuals who would have no memory of me today. My counselor at Wolverine Boys State in 1975 boosted my confidence in ways he will never know. The man who shared his private room with me at a Bahai retreat after I stopped to visit a friend for just a couple of hours but decided to stay for the weekend is someone whose name I have forgotten but whose kindness lives on in my memory.

But what is the legacy of a 28 year old young man who died of an intentional fentanyl overdose?

In *I Never Sang for My Father*, Robert Woodruff Anderson writes that "Death ends a life, but it does not end a relationship, which struggles on in the survivor's mind toward some final resolution, some clear meaning, which it perhaps never finds." As those who knew and loved Nick struggle with the final resolution, there is no doubt that his legacy lives on.

Had Nick not introduced me to *Recovery Dharma*, I would not have written this book, a book that puts you in a relationship with Nick. Although he did not realize a contented sobriety in this lifetime, part of Nick's legacy is the assistance he offers to you on your path to recovery. It is a gift he didn't know he was offering, but it is a gift just the same.

Elements in *Dedicated to Nick Jetton*

The background of this portrait of Nick Jetton incorporates Gustave Klimt's *Farm Garden with Sunflowers* (1907) and Vincent Van Gogh's *Sunflowers in Vase* (1888). A biological sketch of a raspberry created by the Department of Agriculture (1891) is found in the foreground.

Table of Contents

Shortly after I started my Buddhist practice, I came across a quotation incorrectly attributed to the Venerable Ajahn Chah that "If all you had to do is sit, even the chickens would be enlightened." Although Chah did write about chickens, he never made this specific observation. However, the idea that I must take action has influenced by Buddhist practice.

In answering the question of whether one needs to sit for long hours, Chah cites the chicken,

> No, sitting for hours on end is not necessary. Some people think that the longer you can sit, the wiser you must be. I have seen chickens sit on their nests for days on end! Wisdom comes from being mindful in all postures. Your practice should begin as you awaken in the morning. It should continue until you fall asleep. Don't be concerned about how long you can sit. What is important is only that you keep watchful whether you are working or sitting or going to the bathroom.

It is too easy to get so caught up in the performance of rituals that we miss the essence of the practice. We try to do too much and then give up. Bhikkhu Bodi advises that we should not force our practice. Maybe I cannot sit for even fifteen minutes at one time during the day. But maybe I can sit three times for five minutes each or five times during the day for three minutes each.

Journalling, like meditation, is important but should not be forced. There is no requirement that we must spend so much time each day in reflection, that we must answer the "Inquiry Questions" from *Recovery Dharma* in order, or that we have to answer all of them.

There is nothing that stops us from adding some of our own questions or answering a question by designing a piece of art. We can discuss the questions with members of our community as we finish a chapter or even an individual question. Or we can wait until we have finished all our reflections. How we journal is not so important as that we journal.

In his observations on chickens, Chah counsels "Try to be mindful and let things take their natural course." For things to take their natural course requires action. There is no advantage in simply obtaining a copy of *Addiction Recovery Through Buddhist Wisdom* or *Recovery Dharma* and then just sitting on them. Don't just sit on this journal. Reflect on the "Inquiry Questions." Chah might not have said it, but it is still true that, if all we had to do is sit, even the chickens would be enlightened.

Elements in *Table of Contents*

The background is an elongated version of William T. Horton's "A Trip to the Moon" which appeared on the cover of his *A Book of Images* (1898). The hand colored photograph of a lotus created by Ogawa Kazumasa (1896) has a Buddha image sitting in it. Although we know that the woman is Camille Clifford, I am not specifically referencing her. The chickens were uploaded into PixaBay by Scarlet_Letter and GDJ.

Inquiry Questions

When I first reflected on my life as an active alcoholic, I wrote some questions on the top of a blank journal, one question per page. The questions were not mine in that I did not create them, but they were mine to use. When I journal, I generally do not like responding to prompts. But I needed those prompts in early recovery because I didn't know what questions to ask. Because I could not come up with my own questions, I looked to guidance from the many thousands of men and women who had previously recovered from alcoholism. I needed their experience because I didn't have any of my own.

The act of writing out answers to the questions—instead of just thinking about them—is vital because it made it harder for me to fool myself. Writing it down in words makes it real. Furthermore, by forcing myself to put my thoughts in writing, I clarified my thinking.

After the Saturday morning meditation class I attend, I join friends for coffee. We have some rousing discussions of the *dhamma* and the role Buddhism plays in our lives. Although we are following the same path, our paths are very different. I am challenged by their approaches to living the Noble Eightfold Path and use their experiences to improve my understanding of the Buddha *dhamma*. I have a stronger Buddhist practice because of these discussions.

But where I learn the most is not during our time at Café Even. It is when I later write in my journal, where I take time to reflect—in writing—about what we discussed.

My reflections aren't limited to text. Sometimes I sketch ideas for pieces of art, a process I find promotes understanding.

I am grateful to Recovery Dharma Global for publishing their "Inquiry Questions" under a Creative Commons license that allowed me to include them in *Addiction Recovery Through Buddhist Wisdom*. They are well written and encourage us to consider the impact of our addictions on our lives, how we can make amends for our past actions, and how we can live lives of contented sobriety today and into the future.

The "Inquiry Questions" are presented here as they appear in the book *Recovery Dharma*. I encourage you to consult that book for explanation and guidance as you work through these prompts. For a richer understanding of the Buddha *dhamma*, I recommend Bhikku Bodhi's *The Noble Eightfold Path: Way to the End of Suffering*.

Elements in *Inquiry Questions*

The background is the cover for the second edition of *Recovery Dharma: How to Use Buddhist Practices and Principles to Heal the Suffering of Addiction* (2023). The couple reading are my relatives Henry Glasner and Maude Wilcox Glasner. The Buddha is sitting on Robert Thorton's "The Sacred Egyptian Bean" which is plate 31 in his *The Temple of Flora* (1804). Some bushes complete the piece.

The First Noble Truth

The truth of dukkha / pervasive dissatisfaction.

The First Noble Truth is *dukkha*, a Pali word usually translated as "suffering" and is understood to mean that life is filled with suffering. Yet "suffering" is an inadequate translation.

Dukkha does refer to suffering as we typically understand it using the English word, but *dukkha* also refers to sorrow at the death of a loved one or the loss of an item we misplaced. When we are frustrated, we are experiencing *dukkha*. When we are separated from family or friends or need to say our "goodbyes" at the end of a pleasant evening, we experience *dukkha*. *Dukkha* can refer to any specific or even general sense of emptiness or unsatisfactoriness.

Dukkha springs from change. Everything in life is impermanent and change causes dissatisfaction when the attachments we formed to people, places, and things are altered. Change is unavoidable. Nothing is permanent. Therefore, life is *dukkha*.

For me *dukkha* is best understood as a pervasive dissatisfaction.

Because critics of Buddhism focus on the inadequate translation of an untranslatable Pali word, Buddhism is too often viewed as pessimistic. It has even been accused of being nihilistic, that it argues that life is meaningless. Such is not the case. As followers of the Buddha *dhamma*, we can find true happiness but we cannot find it by attaching ourselves to things that are impermanent.

While I was drafting this reflection, I saw a news report concerning a man who was upset because he was forced to pay $5,250 each for four tickets so that his daughter and her three friends could attend a country western concert. Without factoring in the cost of the limousine and clothes and food and other favors, the evening's entertainment cost $21,000 for four people.

When his daughter initially thought that she could not attend the concert, she reported that she went home slamming stuff because she was so disappointed. Even though the young woman and her friends attended the concert, the experience was marred by dissatisfaction. The father suffered. His daughter suffered. Her friends suffered. Others who were involved with them suffered.

The week before this incident took place, one of my students—who I assume makes less money per year than the father paid for one night's entertainment—showed me a t-shirt she had purchased the weekend before. Her excitement was partially attached to an impermanent object that would eventually wear out, but she was mostly excited because she was able to buy the t-shirt with money she had earned, money spent within her means.

I suspect my student felt more joy with her t-shirt than did the young women who attended the concert. Having more, buying more, being attached to more is not conducive to long-term happiness.

It is important to recognize that we cannot escape from the pervasive dissatisfaction that permeates life. But we don't stop with this realization. We recognize *dukkha*, learn where it comes from, understand that it can be removed, and then we follow the Noble Eightfold Path to remove it.

Elements in *The First Noble Truth*

The background is a mosaic from the Baptistry of Florence Duomo, located in Florence, Italy. It was begun in 1225 and was completed sometime in the fourteenth century. The woman is Lily Bart, the heroine of Edith Warton's *The House of Mirth*. She was drawn by A. B. Wenzell for the first edition of the book (1905). The barbed wire was designed by pacahuala and released on Pixabay. The light is taken from Pablo Picaso's *Guernica* painted as a response to the bombing of the Basque town of Guernica. It was first exhibited in the Spanish Pavilion at the 1937 World Fair in Paris.

The Second Noble Truth

The truth of the causes of dukkha / pervasive dissatisfaction.

Shortly after I started practicing the Buddha *dhamma* and long before GPS was a standard feature in cars and on cell phones, I was charged with taking six visiting monks to a Vesak celebration in downtown Detroit. Theravada Buddhists believe that Vesak marks the anniversary of the Gautama Buddha's birth, enlightenment, and death. It is one of the two most important ceremonies in the Theravada tradition.

Unfortunately, a car did not let me merge. As a result, I missed my exit. I was angry at the car's driver who, in retrospect, likely did not even see me trying to change lanes. I was embarrassed because I was lost in the metropolitan area in which I was living. I was worried that the other people at temple would think less of me. I was even irritated at the monk who calmly said, "It's OK. This way we can see more of Detroit." Didn't he realize just how bad getting lost made me look?

At that point, I had been sober for more than 20 years, but I still held tightly to my ego because, as I learned in childhood, I always had to be fine, always be in control, could never make a mistake.

Part of my irritation with the monk was that I wanted the serenity he had. Fifteen years after this incident, I am not so controlled by ego. But when I was delivering monks to a Vesak celebration, I was sober but, with only a fledgling Buddhist practice, I was still angry, irritated, embarrassed, and suffering.

To say that the cause of suffering is a result of our desires and attachments can, in some circumstances, sound like victim blaming. Some of us have had abusive parents or partners or bosses or friends. We have all had people do cruel things to us, take advantage of us, hurt us in so many ways. Yet, ultimately, they are not, outside of some physical manifestations of violence, responsible for our suffering. We suffer because of how we respond to our attachments and to the world around us.

Recognizing that it is our desires and attachments that cause our pervasive dissatisfaction does not excuse those individuals who victimized us. They will live with and be reborn with the *khamma* they created. Where appropriate, Wise Action could mean holding them accountable—legally or otherwise—for the harm they caused. But for our own recovery, instead of focusing on them, we need to see how we contribute to our own suffering and how—regardless of any good intentions—we cause others to suffer.

I used to get very angry when a student or anyone else lied to me. Then, after reading Tich Nhat Hanh's *Anger: Wisdom for Cooling the Flames*, my approach changed and my suffering diminished. Hanh suggests that when someone lies to us, that we approach them as if they were mistaken. This strategy works very well because I don't get angry when people make mistakes. Mistakes happen. Generally, they are unintentional.

Now, when a student makes an error in what they are saying, I don't look to intent. Instead of getting angry, I reply, "I believe that you are mistaken." Then I provide an accurate account supported with appropriate documentation. Why should I let a student or anyone else have control over my serenity and peace of mind?

Hanh's approach does not excuse the other person's behavior or mean that the other person cannot be held accountable. But it does mean that I don't have to make someone else's unwise actions the basis of how I respond to the world.

Elements in *The Second Noble Truth*

The background combines Gustav Klimt's *The Lady in* Gold (1907) with Odilon Redon's *Dream* (1878-1882). In the foreground is Thomas Nast's caricature of Boss Tweed from an editorial cartoon called "The BRAINS" which appeared in *Harper's Weekly* (21 October 1872). Tweed is standing on a Standard oil tank that has been drawn as an eight armed octopus. This lithograph was published by the J. Ottmann Lithograph Company (7 September 1904).

The Third Noble Truth

The truth of the end of dukkha / pervasive dissatisfaction.

After identifying how *dukkha* arises, the Gautama Buddha assures us that we can end pervasive dissatisfaction. All we must do is give up our attachments! Fortunately, he provided the Noble Eightfold Path for us to follow to reach *nibbana*, the end of suffering.

What many people don't realize is that Siddhartha Gautama was not the first person to become a Buddha. We know the names of 27 others who became Buddhas before him. The difference between Siddhartha and the previous Buddhas is that he decided to teach the path toward enlightenment.

One of the reasons that I often refer to the Gautama Buddha instead of just "the Buddha" is to remind myself that I don't have to figure everything out for myself. I have been given a path to follow and others who can assist me along the path.

In Recovery Dharma, support comes from wise friends, a mentor/mentee relationship, practice partners, admirable friends, or an inquiry circle. Many people in Recovery Dharma are also affiliated with Alcoholics Anonymous where they get a sponsor. According to Recovery Dharma, the two groups are not mutually exclusive. In addition to attending meetings, listening to *dhamma* talks, and making friends in recovery programs, we can also look outside Recovery Dharma for guidance.

Having a good therapist has been instrumental in the quality of life I have today. After seeing the same person for seven or so years, some might wonder what value I am getting. Do I really need to still see him? Considering the reasons that took me to therapy, the answer is arguably "No." I no longer suffer acute anxiety attacks. It has been years since I have needed to take antidepressants. I have a very comfortable, serene life. Yet, I still benefit from his support, not as someone who is dependent on my therapist but as someone who wants to continue to grow.

When I first stopped drinking, there was a man of my acquaintance who had been sober about five years. I admired his quality sobriety and he had much to offer me. Over the years, he remained sober but had less and less to offer. Eventually, he had nothing new to teach me about recovery. It is not that his sobriety had decreased. The problem was that he reached a comfortable plateau and stopped growing.

Over the years, I have reached many comfortable plateaus where I could have remained. But I have chosen to continue to grow. In Buddhism, you can be reborn a god, but this is not considered desirable. Yes, gods live comfortable lives, so comfortable that they can be so content that they stop walking the Noble Eightfold Path.

In addition to finding people who can support our recovery journeys, we need to be realistic about what we can offer others. About a month before I began writing this book, a young man asked if I would be his sponsor. I replied "No."

I explained that even though I wrote my dissertation, books, and articles on AA, I do not currently work the Twelve Steps. Nor did I gain recovery from addiction through the Buddha *dhamma* or Recovery Dharma Global. As a sponsor, I had nothing to offer. But, as "Uncle Steve," I welcomed being part of his recovery process.

Within the Buddhist tradition, we enjoy a *sangha* which is a community of believers who support each other. We do not need to walk the Noble Eightfold Path alone.

Elements in *The Third Noble Truth*

The background is Alfred Kubin's *Scène sous-marine* (1906) that has been filtered with a crisscross etching. Although it is difficult to make out, Kubin's underwater scene is of an octopus laying on its back. The lotus is a photograph that was hand colored by Ogawa Kazumasa (1896). Guanyin is the Bodhisattva of compassion.

The Fourth Noble Truth

The truth of the path that leads to the end of suffering which is known as the Eightfold Path.

In the Fourth Noble Truth, the Gautama Buddha gives us the Noble Eightfold Path that leads to the cessation of *dukkha*, the pervasive dissatisfaction that permeates our lives. It is a path that promotes virtue, concentration, and wisdom. The path toward enlightenment avoids extreme measures and provides a middle way between the pursuit of sensual pleasures and self-mortification.

When I first read *Recovery Dharma*, I immediately noticed that the first word of each noble truth was translated as "wise" instead of the more common "right." Therefore, in Recovery Dharma, individuals take "Wise Action" instead of "Right Action."

As someone who had already spent years incorporating the *dhamma* into his life, I understood that what is "right" is that which produces beneficial results. Yet, for someone new to Buddhism, the idea of "right" could be seen as an extreme. If you are not doing something 100% right, you are wrong. There is no middle way in the right/wrong dichotomy as it is expressed in many aspects of popular culture or by religious extremists. By moving away from the right/wrong dichotomy, we can better concentrate on the path itself.

My lived experience as a Theravada Buddhist is that the Noble Eightfold Path is the best way to remove attachments and cravings and suffering from my life. But, to use common American terms, I do not want to say that other paths are necessarily wrong.

Following the Noble Eightfold Path will result in a life of contented sobriety. I do not believe that it is the only path toward sobriety, but I know that it works. Nor do I want to say that I am a bad Buddhist or bad person because I still have attachments and cravings and suffering.

Bhikkhu Bodhi explains that "To follow the Noble Eightfold Path is a matter of practice rather than intellectual knowledge, but to apply the path correctly, it has to be properly understood." We need to study the Buddha *dhamma* in order to live the Buddha *dhamma*. Yet study—without practice—cannot lead to a cessation of pervasive dissatisfaction or help us on our quest toward recovery.

It would be 36 years after I stopped drinking that the *Recovery Dharma* prompts were published. A Buddhist recovery path was not available to me when I decided to stop drinking. Therefore, I located a list of prompts designed by a different recovery program. I wrote each prompt on the top of a page in a journal and then flipped back and forth between the pages while reflecting on them.

There will be people who pick up this journal—or any other journal—and not write one word in it. This is a mistake. While it is possible to stop drinking without self-reflection, I do not believe we can gain contentment without it.

In my early research into Alcoholics Anonymous, I came across the phrase "non-drinking, non-recovered alcoholic" to describe the person who simply stops drinking but does not follow the steps of recovery. As a Buddhist, I could follow the fifth precept of not consuming mind altering substances and still live a life of active suffering if I don't take the time to reflect.

Elements in *The Fourth Noble Truth*

Three images were combined for this piece: Tsukioka Yoshitoshi's woodcut *Miki Toyokichi Educating Himself and Fellow Prisoners* (April 1875), Sekine Untei's illustration of sea creatures(19th century), and Alfred Kubin's *Scène sous-marine* (1906) which includes an octopus. A statue of the Gautama Buddha is in the center.

Wise Understanding

When I was younger, before starting out on a trip, we would consult a map or get directions from a friend. We would not just get into our car and begin to aimlessly drive. Even with the advent of GPS, we can be led astray if we don't have a general understanding of our direction, as happened to me on a recent trip where GPS wanted to add miles and miles of extra driving to my route. I have even read of cases such as the one where a person drove their car into a lake because that is the route they had been given by GPS. We need to have some understanding of our direction before we begin our trip.

Our path to contented sobriety is similar. We know our destination, but we need directions on how to get there. Without directions we stumble about taking wrong turns, getting lost, or even abandoning the trip entirely. Some recovery programs are like the maps I consulted in my youth. They have specific steps one must follow. You first drive so far down one road before making a turn onto another one. The Noble Eightfold Path is not like that. We simultaneously work on all aspects of the path. Yet, we must begin somewhere and that somewhere is Wise Understanding.

As we begin our journey, it is helpful to know that the path is broken into three general categories: bodily actions, verbal actions, and mental actions. Bodily actions include not destroying life, not taking what is not freely given, and avoiding unwise conduct when it comes to sensual pleasures. The verbal actions address false speech, slanderous speech, harsh speech, and idle chatter. The mental actions focus on covetousness, ill will, and unwise views.

Yet, a Wise Understanding of the path does not require that we have a full understanding of all aspects of the path.

In most of my life, I am an incredible geek and intellectual. I spend hours researching topics. Recently, while working on another book, I decided to include a reference to hospitality in the Islamic tradition. I had already done extensive reading about hospitality but read an additional ten articles—some published in scholarly journals—before writing the one sentence in the book that references Islamic hospitality. This sentence might not even be included in the finished book. Yet, even after I had more information than I needed, I continued to read before writing that one sentence.

The one area in my life where I do not geek out on research is my Buddhist practice. I did not try to read everything written about the Noble Eightfold Path before practicing it in my life. I do read the *suttas* and commentaries and books and articles written by Buddhist teachers and scholars so that I have Wise Understanding. But I focus on my practice. My focus is on "How can I apply what I read to my practice?" instead of gathering knowledge for its own sake. Simply citing *suttas* will not the mark of Wise Understanding.

When I consulted maps, I did not need to know the weather conditions and traffic patterns and where road signs and stop lights and gas stations were located before starting my trip. My understanding of the path could develop while driving it. Wise Understanding of the Noble Eightfold Path is to know that the path is there and that it will lead to a contented life of sobriety free from pervasive dissatisfaction. That is enough to begin.

Elements in *Wise Understanding*

The background is my *Lorain's Apple Orchard* (2020), one of more than 20 portraits I did of my father during the past few months of his life. The original piece included my father's chest showing the scar from his heart surgery. At the foot of the tree is Unionville High School which my father attended and at which he later taught. The ground was a photograph I took of some landscape as I was driving to visit him a couple weeks before his death. The apple which is duplicated in different sizes was released by Capri23auto on Pixabay. To the original piece, I added some more of Capri23auto's apples at the base of the tree as well as three versions of a rotten apple that Kasman released on Pixabay. The books were released on Pixabay by anaterate which is also where Clker-Free-Vector-Images released the image of the barbed wire. The raspberry is a botanical sketch which is part of the U.S. Department of Agriculture Pomological Watercolor Collection (1891).

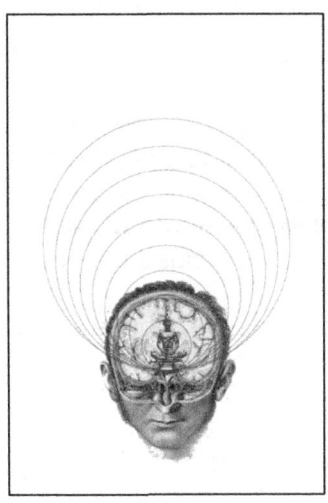

Wise Intention

Our actions always follow from our intentions, so it is important that we have a Wise Understanding of them. Because it is so easy to deceive ourselves, putting our thoughts in writing or some other fixed form and then sharing our reflections with a trusted friend or mentor helps ensure that we act with Wise Intention.

I mention other fixed forms—a term from copyright law that only a research geek would use—because creating art is how I often study concepts. Others might compose music or create a dance.

While creating the piece of art that illustrates this chapter, I struggled to understand various aspects of Wise Intention. There were drafts and revisions and false starts before I settled on the final illustration. The process of creating the art was more important in my path to contented sobriety and eventual enlightenment than the actual finished piece. The same can be said for journaling. It is the process that helps us develop Wise Understanding of our intentions, intentions that are not always wise.

As the story of Cakkhupāla illustrates, in Buddhist teaching, *kamma* is based on intention. Cakkhupāla was a blind monk who, while walking in meditation, accidentally killed some insects. He did not receive bad *kamma* for violating the First Precept that we should refrain from taking life because he had no intention of killing.

But to simply proclaim our intentions is not sufficient. For example, having empathy for someone is essentially meaningless unless our feeling of empathy causes us to act with compassion.

As a Buddhist, I wish that all sentient beings be well, be happy, and be at peace. The *Karaniya Metta Sutta* which provides a foundation for acts of loving kindness tells me how to make this Wise Intention a reality.

First, we begin with ourselves. Then, we reflect on our intention that people close to us—people with whom we already have kind and loving relationships—are well, happy, and peaceful. Then we expand our intention that those with whom we work and associate but with whom we don't have close relationships are well, happy, and peaceful.

Next, we consider people who have done us harm. Instead of wishing harm to them, we wish that they be well, that they be happy, and that they be peaceful. Eventually, we spread our intention to the entire world, to all sentient beings. This is difficult but necessary because intentions govern actions. If my intention is to have a healthy, happy, and peaceful life for myself, I need to have the same Wise Intention for others.

When it comes to wishing well for those who have harmed us, we need to remember that wishing well is not the same as excusing unacceptable behavior. When I shared my home with a paranoid narcissist, I wanted him to move out, but it was not my intention for him to suffer any more pain than he was already suffering. His life was filled with pervasive dissatisfaction. What good would it do me to wish him further ill will? Increasing his *dukkha* does not make my life any more happy, healthy, and peaceful.

If I intend harm to anyone, even those who have harmed me, my actions will be harmful to me.

Elements in *Wise Intention*

Nicolas-Henri Jacob's frontal cross-section of the encephalon was published as plate 25 in Claude Bernard and Jean-Marc Bourgery's *Traité complet de l'anatomie de l'homme,* vol. 3 (1867-1871). The meditator was released on Pixaby by eugeniohansenofs. The circles were inspired by the *Karaniya Metta Sutta.*

Making Amends

Our purpose in confronting our past in a realistic way is so that we can learn from our mistakes and then amend/change the way we live our lives.

I do not want to minimize the importance of apologizing for our behavior, of taking responsibility for the ways that we have harmed others. Yet it is not the apology that is most important. It is doing what we can to right the wrongs we committed and then changing our behaviors so that we do not cause similar harm in the future.

I once had someone approach me to make what is called a Nineth Step Amends as part of their twelve step recovery program. This is someone who, from what I could observe, was practicing the same behaviors that had so damaged the relationship I had with them. I hope that taking this action eventually led to a long lasting recovery for them. But in terms of repairing our broken relationship, it was a performance lacking meaning. Because they didn't change their behavior, repairing the damage was not accomplished.

Something that can be difficult to face is when the harm we do is unintentional or caused by a mental health issue. In my late 50s, I was diagnosed with schizoid personality disorder which helped explain some of the difficulties I had in maintaining relationships. As someone with schizoid personality disorder, it is difficult for me to express a full range of emotions or to show much interest or ability to form relationships with others.

As a professor, my disorder often benefits my students because I did not get caught up in the drama of their lives which makes it easier for me to help them. But the inability to show emotions well is a problem in most relationships.

As someone who is interested in increasing the quality of his sobriety along with his Buddhist practice, I cannot ask others to excuse certain behaviors by claiming that "Because I have schizoid personality disorder, there is nothing else I can do." There are things I can do.

A few days before drafting this reflection, I was extremely dismissive of a young man I hired to weed my flowerbeds. He had finished a big project and asked if I wanted to see it. Initially, I replied that I didn't need to check his work. But that was not really what he wanted. He already knew he had done a good job. He didn't need me to tell him that. Instead, he had completed a big job and was proud of his work. He wanted me to experience sympathetic joy by sharing his success with me.

Fortunately, I was able to realize my error and let him show me his accomplishment. Because I have reflected on past relationships and have worked with a psychologist on how to change my behavior, my disorder does not control my life as it once did.

I have been sober long enough that most people have not experienced me as an active alcoholic. Those who knew me before 23 March 1983 have seen the changes that have come with sobriety and have accepted my amends. Our relationships have been repaired like kintsugi pottery, a process that doesn't try to hide the breaks where the broken pottery is mended back together. Instead, kintsugi celebrates the imperfections with gold or silver or platinum lacquer. Like a kintsugi bowl, many of those repaired relationships are more beautiful than the original.

Elements in *Making Amends*

The background is Maria Sibylla Merian's watercolor of a branch of *Duroia eriopila* with a Zebra Swallowtail Butterfly (*Eurytides proesilaus*) and the larva and pupa of the Melantho Tigerwing Butterfly (*Xanthocleis psidii*). The watercolor was published in her *Metamorphosis Insectorum Surinamensium* (1705). Arthur Rothstein took the photograph of the abandoned farm in Cimarron County, Oklahoma (April 1936). It was taken as part of his work with the Farm Service Administration. The Kintsugi bowl with spoon is an ink wash from a Hokusai School Sketchbook and has been attributed to Katsushika Hokusa (c. 1830-1850).

Wise Speech

What is my real intention when I speak? If I feel the need to explain in advance that my comments are not meant to be offensive, I must consider if I have thought about them well enough to speak my thoughts compassionately. If I begin a comment with "I don't mean to be offensive or upset you," I must consider whether my real intent is to cause harm because I am angry or for some other reason.

If you feel a burning desire to tell someone something for their own good, your motive is likely not Wise Speech. Or, if you are delighted to think of the perfect verbal response you wish you could have used in a conversation that ended hours earlier, you can be pretty sure that there was little perfect about your delightful response if your goal is to practice Wise Speech.

The Noble Eightfold Path is not designed in the way I scaffold major assignments for my students where you complete one task before moving on to the next. Instead, the Noble Eightfold Path is more like the arms of octopuses which are some of the most flexible limbs found in nature. All arms work simultaneously together to accomplish their goal. As such, Wise Intention is needed to evaluate Wise Speech.

Recently, an acquaintance in early recovery made a decision that was not particularly thoughtful. For their own good, I do need to bring up the incident so that they don't repeat it in the future. But I don't need to bring it up today. Or tomorrow. Or even next week. For their own good, they need to know that what they did was problematic. I will discuss the situation with them eventually. The only reason to bring up the situation immediately would be to vent my own irritation because I didn't appreciate what they did. To bring it up now would make it all about me and how I was irritated with them. That is neither compassionate to them nor the foundation for Wise Speech.

Idle chatter can be a form of unwise speech even if we try to define it as "bonding." When we meet someone new, we might engage in casual conversation to get to know them better and to build relationships, something that could be considered Wise Speech. But engaging in gossip rather than bridge building is not.

I find it easy to deceive myself when it comes to intention. That is why it is so important to reflect in my journal and to discuss my intentions with others. In the past, I have argued that venting, when done behind closed doors with a trusted friend can be beneficial, essentially a form of Wise Speech. But as I have developed in my Buddhist practice, I am not so sure. While I am not willing to totally disavow some benefits of venting, I am not sure that it can ever be practiced with true Wise Intention. There are less destructive ways of getting something off my chest than in the types of venting I did in the past.

Honesty requires me to admit that I still vent in ways that I don't think are consistent with Wise Intention. But my vents are becoming more tempered so that I can really investigate the issues at hand. Extreme venting is a reflection of my mental well-being and has little to do with how others have treated me.

I remember when a monk expressed sorrow at the recent death of his grandmother. He told me that she had been a good woman and had had a good rebirth. Yet, he concluded, "I am still human."

I am not a terrible person or a failure at contented sobriety or Buddhist practice because I still vent or practice other speech that is less than wise. I do my best to practice Wise Intention which leads to Wise Speech. I often fall short because I am still human, a human committed to improving his Buddhist practice. And I continue to improve.

Elements in *Wise Speech*

The background is William Hogarth's etching *Characters and Caricaturas* (1743). The false prophets with frogs coming out of their mouths is a commentary on Revelation 16:13 and was published in *The Queen Mary Apocalypse* (c. 1300s). The woman was created by Prawny and released on Pixabay.

Wise Action

Wise Action primarily focuses on three of the Five Precepts: abstaining from taking life, abstaining from taking what is not given, and abstaining from sexual impropriety. Because killing, stealing, and sexual conduct are covered in the Five Precepts, one might wonder why we need to have Wise Action. Isn't that redundant?

The "redundancy" allows us to gain new perspectives on the *dhamma*. For example, as Bhikkhu Bodhi writes in his analysis of Wise Action in *The Noble Eightfold Path*, the transgression of taking what is not given implies "withholding from others what should rightfully be given to them." When action is required, the fact that "I didn't do anything" could mean that I acted unwisely.

I would not be speaking truthfully if I said that I like all my students. I don't. Some are terribly annoying or worse. How does this relate to Wise Action?

Let's assume that a student I don't like wanted to meet with me outside my office hours. If I would generally be available to students during the time they wanted to meet, Wise Action mandates that I meet with them. I am not contractually required to meet with a student outside my office hours, but withholding from the student what they should rightfully be given is not acceptable. The fact that I don't care for the student is not a factor in how I treat them. If I am available to students during certain times of the day, I am available to all students.

I have a memorable student from more than two decades ago, an individual whose lack of social skills made him universally disliked. His actions caused people to avoid him, something I would have preferred to do as well. But in my dealings with him, I practiced Wise Action even before I started to follow the Buddha *dhamma*. As a result, he ended up enrolling in four classes I taught. I was his favorite professor, a professor who he never figured out didn't like him.

In considering Wise Actions, we can think about other times we withhold something that should be rightfully given. The concept of *caveat emptor*—or buyer beware—does not absolve me from withholding information about mechanical problems to the buyer of my used car. As an employee, I cannot loaf and withhold work from my employer. As an employer, I cannot withhold safe working conditions and fair pay from my employees if I want to act wisely.

The people with whom I share my life deserve certain considerations. I am not practicing Wise Action if I withhold my time from them because I am so caught up with work or ignore them for my own pleasurable pursuits and hobbies.

If I am on a dating website and withhold the fact that I am married, it is both a lack of Wise Action and a violation of the Third Precept which requires that we refrain from sexual misconduct. Such infidelity is obvious, but it might not be so obvious that I am not practicing Wide Action if I withhold the fact that I am not interested in establishing a long-term relationship when I know that this is the goal of someone who pursues me.

As a person who is interested in recovery, I must look at my actions and how they impact others. But I must also consider how my lack of action impacts others.

Elements in *Wise Action*

The portrait of the woman churning butter and reading was taken by J.W. Dunn (1897). His copyright mark is in the lower right corner. The background is an agricultural calendar showing work performed each month and is from a manuscript of Pietro Crescenzi (c. 1306). The octopus is from James Sowerby's *The British Miscellany, or, Coloured Figures of New, Rare, or Little Known Animal Subjects - Many Not Before Ascertained to be Inhabitants of the British Isles - and Chiefly in the Possession of the Author* (1806). The lotus is a hand-colored photograph created by Ogawa Kazumasa (1896). The final element is a statue of the Gautama Buddha.

The First Precept

To refrain from taking life.

As someone who once kept the telephone number for the suicide prevention hot line taped to the wall next to his desk, I am keenly aware that the idea of taking life—even one's own—is not a philosophical concept limited to intellectual discourses. For Christians, suicide is the one unpardonable sin. Buddhists believe that while suicide might end the suffering in this life, the suffering will continue into the next. Existentialists such as Albert Camus validate suicide as a reasonable response to the absurdity of human existence. Others see suicide as a mental health issue.

What is too often missing from such learned discussions is the fact that suicide is extremely personal. Had I used the razor blade I kept in my wallet to slice my wrists—lengthwise, not across—when I was 18 years old, I would not have been thinking of those who survived me, those who would have struggled for some final resolution. Blinded by my own suffering, I would not have realized that ending my life did not end the relationships others had with me.

I do not remember how I ended up in a restaurant drinking black coffee instead of committing suicide, but, years later, I still needed to keep the suicide prevention number close at hand. And this was after I have been sober for a few years.

I suspect that few of us involved in recovery have not been impacted by someone who killed themselves or died as a direct result of their addiction. Many of us have failed when we tried to commit suicide ourselves and others miraculously ended up drinking black coffee instead of being a suicide statistic.

Those of us who have experienced someone else's death are left with unresolved issues, survivor's guilt, or a host of other emotions as we try to come to a resolution that we might never find.

I realize that discussions of the First Precept do not generally focus on taking our own lives or how to process our emotions when confronted with a loved one who did.

For me, the precepts encourage me to push past the superficial to consider how I might support killing. In 2009, I had the honor of sponsoring the Katina Ceremony held at the Great Lakes Buddhist Vihara. The night before the ceremony, over 100 people crammed into my home to participate in a Pirith chanting ceremony for which my brother prepared venison stew from a deer he had shot. My brother and I joked that my serving the stew was acceptable because he had not killed the deer for me or for my guests. Yet, had I not hosted the chanting, would the deer have died?

In this case, the answer is "Yes." My brother would have killed the deer to have meat for his family. Arguably, he was acting with generosity by sharing his food with us. But, when I go to my wonderful halal butcher, can I say the same thing about the lamb I buy? As one individual, my purchasing lamb does not affect the marketplace. But would it not be better if I adopted a vegetarian diet? I do not consider myself a hypocrite when I answer "Yes, it would be" while also having no plan to become vegetarian.

Although it might not be an approach shared by my monks, I continue to push myself to consider how I am indirectly violating precepts by the choices I make. Even if I am not in technical violation, does a precept point to a better way for me to conduct my life? How does the First Precept relate to my personal choices that reflect climate change for example. In early sobriety, I need not worry about these more complex questions. But the Buddha *dhamma* and the Noble Eightfold Path continue to serve me as I grow in both recovery and spiritual direction.

Elements in *The First Precept*

The background is Gustave Doré's "The Creation of Light" which was created for *La Grande Bible de Tours* (1866). In the foreground is a hand-colored albumen silver print of Kazumasa Ogawa's wood carving of a man killing an octopus. This photograph was published in *Japan. Described and Illustrated by the Japanese* (1897) which was edited by Captain F. Brinkley. The horse is a detail from Pablo Picasso's *Guernica* (1937). An image of the Buddha encircled by a halo sits on the horse's head.

The Second Precept

__To refrain from taking what is not freely given.__

I have a colleague who is also a personal friend of mine. On some mornings before my first class, I enjoy sitting in her office chatting over a cup of coffee. Sometimes she will come to my office during the break between her classes. These are mutually enjoyable experiences.

When we think about taking what is not freely given, we typically do not consider the theft of time. What makes the exchanges between my colleague and I agreeable is that we generally inquire if now is a good time for conversation. I ask if she has time for coffee because I don't want to steal time she needs to prepare for her classes, to take from her time that is not freely given.

Another colleague visits me during my office hours, a time when I make myself available to students. When a student arrives, my colleague immediately stops talking to me so that I can engage with the student. Often, she will leave my office so as not to steal time from the student.

It has only been during the past couple of years that I have focused on how I had too often taken people's time when it was not freely given. I wanted to talk or have coffee or otherwise engage and did so without considering whether the interaction was stealing time that they needed to use for something else.

Just because someone doesn't tell me to go away doesn't mean that they are freely giving their time. I know that I have allowed people to steal my time because I was "too polite" to say otherwise.

Even more recently, I have become more focused on what I allow to steal my time: social media, entertainment, texting with friends, other people. It is not that any of these actions are unwise in and of themselves, but they might not be wise to the extent that I do them.

Typically, I only practice the Five Precepts each day, but I try to keep in mind that one of the Eight Precepts—abstaining from dancing, singing, music shows, wearing garlands, and beautifying with cosmetics—suggests non-sentient things that can steal my time if I am not careful. Before doing something, I might ask myself "Does this entertainment contribute to my life or has it become an obsession that steals my time?" Wise Intention and Wise Action can play roles in answering this question so that I don't fool myself by giving the answer I want to hear.

Although my reflections do not typically address the art itself, the piece of art illustrating the Second Precept serves as a cautionary tale. What was published is not what was initially designed. Instead of the man on the turtle, I had included a man on a snail. While verifying references to include in the description below, I discovered that I had accidentally incorporated the work of another artist, work still covered by United States copyright law. I had not intended to steal her work when I designed the illustration, but had I published the original piece without her permission, I not only would have violated the Second Precept, I would have broken the law.

Wise Action requires that I verify what I "know" to be true because memory is faulty. For example, I must verify the truth expressed in a meme or Tick Tock or other social media before I forward the post to others. If I don't take the action of verifying the information, I cannot absolve myself from bad *kamma* by arguing I had passed on misinformation in ignorance.

Our memories are faulty, as mine was in the case of where the man on the snail image originated, and we can easily deceive ourselves if we are not careful. This is one of the reasons why we journal and talk with trusted friends and mentors.

Elements in *The Second Precept*

Both the background and the tree were designed by geralt and released on Pixabay. The turtle is from Ludwig Heinrich Bojanus' Anatome Testudinis Europaeae (c. 1819-21). I know nothing about the man riding the turtle except when the photograph was taken (c. 1880s).

The Third Precept

To refrain from sensuous misconduct.

From an ethical point of view, the purpose of the Third Precept is to protect marital relationships from outside interference as well as to promote trust within the relationship. The Gautama Buddha took care to define who are illicit sexual partners. We ought not have sexual relations with someone who is married or engaged. We ought not to have sex with someone who is a close relative, under a vow of celibacy, or forbidden by convention. In addition to illicit partners, there is illicit conduct. For example, it is a violation of the precept to have forced sex with someone.

If we do not practice Wise Mindfulness, it is easy to fool ourselves when it comes to intent. For example, one could believe that "The person I am sexually interested in isn't married to their partner, so it doesn't violate the precept if I pursue a relationship with them." It does. Lack of a marriage certificate does not change the commitment of fidelity.

We might also fall into the trap of legalism. "The Buddha teaches that, as a man, I cannot have sex with a married woman. But he doesn't say that I cannot have sex with a married man." He doesn't. But I can't.

When it comes to evaluating my sexual conduct, I look at the honesty involved. As a single person, I could still violate this precept by having sexual relationships with someone who was not illicit if I lie to them about my intent. If my intent is to remain single but I tell someone that I am looking for a long-term relationship, my conduct violates the Third Precept whether or not I engage in sexual activity with them.

But what is the measure of sexual activity? I remember reading about people who consider themselves to be virgins because they have "only" had oral sex. If I "only" have oral sex with a married person who is not my spouse, I violate the Third Precept.

I would even go so far as to suggest that I violate the Third Precept if I allow my partner or potential partner to deceive themselves. Although I am theoretically open to the possibility of entering into a committed relationship or being married, that is not my current desire. I would not be surprised if I remain single for the remainder of my life. That is why I wouldn't date someone whose overwhelming desire is to find a life partner.

Even when I have been totally honest about my intentions, the other person too often denies the reality or thinks that if they are patient that they will change me. I cannot absolve myself from moral responsibility to a relationship that is not rooted in honesty, even when the dishonesty is the result of someone else's denial.

Finally, I need to practice Wise Action by not withholding important information to the other person. For example, one of the factors that contributes to my diagnosis of schizoid personality disorder is a lack of sexual interest. A potential partner needs to know what they can and cannot expect from me. I don't need to mention this on the first date, but it needs to be addressed early.

The fact that I am a research geek can also be a factor indirectly related to the Third Precept and directly related to my personality disorder. My potential partner needs to know that there will be some ways I will be emotionally unavailable. Working with my therapist, I continue to become better with social cues, but my partner needs to be told specifically how I am a work in progress.

By using "sensuous misconduct" rather than "sexual activity" as the translation for the Third Precept, I intend to imply that non-sexual sensuous activity needs to be considered. A popular cliché argues that we can never have too much of a good thing. Yet, we can. We avoid anything taken to the extreme.

Elements in *The Third Precept*

In the foreground are a couple photographed by Wilhelm von Gloeden for *National Geographic* (c. 1880). The background is a detail from Hieronymus Bosch's *The Garden of Earthly Delights* (c. 1480-1505) to which a filter has been applied. Tanaka Yuho's *Kogei Shinzu* (1892) completes the piece.

The Fourth Precept

To refrain from false speech.

In c. 1910, Harold Cazneaux was not the first person to take a self portrait. That distinction goes to Robert Cornelius who, in 1839, produced the world's first portrait. But Cazneaux not only took a portrait, he took what we now call a "selfie." It is an honest look at himself that is preserved for posterity.

When it comes to avoiding false speech, I am generally pretty good at knowing when I am being dishonest with other people. The problem comes in being honest with myself. Sometimes, I don't want to take a hard look at myself because I don't care for what the selfie shows. During my drinking days and even into sobriety, I have treated people terribly. I am embarrassed by behaviors I practiced and have since done my best to make amends to people by apologizing when it was both possible and appropriate. I then continue to make amends by changing the way I live.

For example, I was far too long prone to self-destructive anger and feelings of self-righteousness. It was only after I did some serious reflection that included writing in my journal, reading books such as Thich Nhat Han's *Anger: Wisdom for Cooling the Flames*, and talking with my therapist that I have seen anger radically diminish from my life to the point where I rarely feel angry anymore. Note, I did not say "never." I am on the path to *nibbana*, I have not yet reached enlightenment.

I find that journaling is an important tool to avoid false speech, to keep me honest with myself. When I write in my journal, something I do virtually every day, I can feel when what I am writing isn't true. Because I grew up in a household where I was constantly told that what I felt or believed or experienced wasn't true, questioning my motives comes naturally to me. I don't get this same sense when I just think about a topic or talk with someone else about it.

This does not mean that we shouldn't talk to others. Although it comes naturally for me to question myself, what is natural isn't always easy and the results aren't always accurate. I often ponder about something too long before taking Wise Action. Furthermore, because of my upbringing, I am not always sure if my response to a situation is accurate and need to seek out advice.

Once I asked my therapist how other people who, like me, shared life with an abusive, paranoid narcissist. How did they live in such a relationship? He looked and me and calmly replied, "They don't." Those two words, calmly stated, began the process where I stopped lying to myself about the reality of my situation. None of the reasons I thought I had to stay in the relationship were valid. I was engaging in false speech with myself.

The "Inquiry Questions" published in *Recovery Dharma* and reprinted in this book help us to become honest with ourselves. It is worth taking the time to journal about them and then discussing our thoughts with a trusted friend, mentor, or therapist.

Elements in *The Fourth Precept*

The focal point is a selfie taken by Harold Cazneaux (c. 1910). The background is a photograph taken by my ophthalmologist of the inside of my eye showing a newly developed cataract (26 May 2023). The montage in the corner includes an etching of a flayed man holding his own skin which is attributed to artist Gaspar Becerra and engraver Nicholas Neatrizet and published in Juan de Valverde de Amusco's *Historia de la composicion del cuerpo humano (*1556). The lotus is a photograph that was hand colored by Ogawa Kazumasa (1896). The man in the bottle was published in Richard Penlake's *Trick Photography: A Handbook Describing All the Most Mysterious Photographic Tricks* (1906).

The Fifth Precept

*To refrain from alcohol
and other intoxicants that cloud the mind.*

I clearly remember the day when Sri Lankan monk Bhante Muditha first showed me the Five Precepts. When we came to the fifth precept, he mentioned that this one was often difficult for Westerners. I replied, "Not for me!" I had already been sober for more than 20 years. Yet I know that stopping the use of mind altering substances is not easy even for those who are not addicted to them.

When I stopped drinking, the quality of my life became worse. I was confronted with a new world and had neither the alcohol nor the skills I learned in sobriety to navigate it. The pervasive dissatisfaction that had always been there increased. My early sobriety was one of extreme hand tremors and stuttering as I tried to cope with my anxiety. Yet, I stopped drinking.

I am not sure why anyone who is addicted to alcohol or other drugs stops using these substances, especially during that early period of sobriety. Although I did not relapse, I am not surprised that relapse is so common. But, somehow, I knew that if I stuck it out and endured the white-knuckle sobriety that the gift of contented sobriety would come to me. It has.

Slowly I would learn skills to maintain my sober life. Some were practical. If you are at an event where wine is being served, turn your wine glass upside down. That way someone can't fill it. Others involved reflecting on aspects of my addiction in ways similar to answering Recovery Dharma's "Inquiry Questions." Each year of sobriety, the quality of my life improved.

People often ask why I converted to Buddhism. My answer is that I didn't really convert. While reading about Buddhism for an academic project, I realized that the Buddha *dhamma* expressed what I already believed but didn't have the vocabulary to discuss. I then found a home at the Great Lakes Buddhist Vihara, a temple that primarily serves an expatriate community from Sri Lanka. Because involvement with the community seemed so natural, friends now joke that I must have been Sri Lankan—and Buddhist—in a previous life.

I did not find recovery through Buddhism nor have I used Buddhism to maintain my recovery. Practicing the Fifth Precept is simply part of my daily practice at which I don't have to work. Yet the quality of my life in sobriety has improved since I began my Buddhist practice, a quality of life that would quickly evaporate if I were to stop working the Fifth Precept.

Although the Fifth Precept invites me to consider how my addiction impacted my life, it also invites me to consider whether my use of caffeine violates the Fifth Precept. Sometimes it does. While I might not need to practice the Fifth Precept perfectly in terms of my caffeine consumption, I know that I cannot consume anything that comes into the commonly accepted definition of "alcohol and other drugs."

Are there never exceptions? Buddhism avoids extremes so I have used prohibited substances medicinally. When I had hernia surgery in 2022, I didn't say, "No pain killers for me because I want to practice the Fifth Precept." Although I didn't need to use them, I took the prescribed opiates home with me. The Fifth Precept does not require that I suffer pain after surgery.

In the past, I have been prescribed anti-anxiety and anti-depressant medications and took them as long as needed. Some people need to take mind altering medications for the rest of their lives. Wise Action suggests we should take our prescriptions.

As a recovered alcoholic, this is the precept I must be most vigilant about keeping. If I lose sobriety, I lose everything.

Elements in *The Fifth Precept*

The focus is a Parisian woman in her cannabis garden (1915). The background is Utagawa Hiroshige's *The Plum Garden at Kameido Shrine* (1857) with some green marijuana plants created by cytis and released on Pixabay. In the foreground is the tintype *Discarded Vices* (c. 1860-1880) and a syringe created by quiono and released on Pixabay.

Wise Livelihood

    I live in a world where people drink. I sobered up in an apartment where I had roommates who drank. I know that having alcohol in their home is not possible for everyone in recovery, but after I became sober, I maintained a well-stocked bar for family and friends—until I began my Buddhist practice. Even before I had a deeper appreciation for the Noble Eightfold Path, I decided that if I truly believed that consuming alcohol or other drugs is harmful, I cannot supply them for other people. I didn't realize it at the time, but I was incorporating the spirit of Wise Livelihood into my life.

    Producing and selling alcohol is one of the prohibited occupations that the Gautama Buddha specifically mentions. I wasn't technically producing or selling alcohol when I supplied drinks to my guests, but my actions were not consistent with Wise Livelihood.

    Although the Gautama Buddha does not prevent me from purchasing meat from my Halal butcher[3], I still struggle with the ethics of eating meat. I do have a great deal of gratitude that my butcher has chosen an occupation that allows me to enjoy my lamb and goat. Each Eid al-Fitr and other important Muslim holidays, I bring special gifts to him and the others who work in the shop.

---

    [3] Food sensitivities prevent me from eating beef and chicken so I buy meat from my halal butcher because he sells lamb and goat, two meats I cannot purchase in my local chain groceries. Some people favor halal and kosher meat because they require that animals be killed humanely.

As a professor, I am in an occupation that is not forbidden. This does not mean that I automatically enjoy Wise Livelihood. If I don't give my students the time they deserve or if I advance my career through trickery, I am not following what is expected of someone on the Noble Eightfold Path.

I have always maintained that volunteerism is work experience. As such, I consider how Wise Livelihood applies to the volunteer work I do. Arguably, it is better to do good work for the wrong reasons rather than to not do the good work at all. But do I have Wise Intentions? And, if I don't, how will that affect my performance.

As I draft this book, I am in the last year of my presidency of a statewide organization, a position for which I have stayed one year too long. I find it difficult to keep up my enthusiasm and find that I am just doing the minimum to get by. It is hard to admit that I am not doing the quality work that Wise Livelihood entails. The members of the organization should expect more of me and I expect more of myself. Fortunately, I am taking Wise Action and leaving this position.

Wise Livelihood, for me, requires that I consider my investments and purchases. Does my retirement portfolio make money because I am invested in the manufacture of alcohol or guns?

I also consider how I spend the benefits I receive from my livelihood. I make much more money than survival requires. How do I spend the excess? Supporting scholarships for students is one way. Making charitable donations and providing support for others is another. But how many pairs of shoes do I really need?

I know that some of the questions I ask in this book might not be directly related to the Buddhist ideas that inspire them. But to maintain a better sobriety and Buddhist practice, I allow my mind to contemplate how the arms of the octopus are both independent and interrelated.

Elements in *Wise Livelihood*

The image in the background is a butcher shop published in Ibn Butlan of Baghdad's *Tacuinum Sanitatis* (15th century). The middle image is a late nineteenth-century photograph showing a woman washing laundry reportedly close to Fifteenth Street in Augusta, Georgia. The final featured image is Dr. Christopher James Davis, a British-Barbadian physician who was the first graduate of African descent at Aberdeen University in Scotland. The flower behind Davis is a hand colored photograph of a lotus created by Ogawa Kazumasa (1896).

Wise Effort

In my social media, variations of a parable frequently appear concerning a grandfather who tells his grandson that there are two wolves fighting inside each of us: one good, one evil. When the grandson asks which wolf wins, his grandfather replies, "The one you feed."

During the Summer of 2023, I was working to complete two books, this one and one I had started months earlier. Which one did I finish first? This one. Why? Because that is the one I fed, the one where I put my energy. If, sometime in the future, you look for a list of my publications, I am hopeful that you will discover that the other book has been published, too. But it won't happen if I don't put effort into it.

Energy is the mental factor behind effort. Effort can be used wisely or unwisely. We determine where we put our effort. Where we put our effort determines both the quality of our recovery and the quality of our Buddhist practice.

As I was drafting this chapter, I know someone who had a setback in terms of their recovery. Because it is their story and not mine to tell, I won't go into details other than to say that they didn't return to drug use after this setback.

This individual was early in recovery and had a weak understanding of the Buddha *dhamma*. Yet they practiced Wise Effort in a skillful fashion. They could have fed the feeling that they were a worthless person who didn't deserve recovery. This person has done that before, as have many of us. They also might do it again. But this time, they put their effort into reaching out for help and taking Wise Actions. Their sober foundation remained shaky yet firm and will continue to get firmer if they continue to take Wise Effort. A few days after their crisis, this person passed a pre-employment drug test.

Because they made an understandable yet misguided decision, their day started out badly. Had they not engaged in Wise Effort, their future could have become suddenly bleak.

Sometimes, unwise effort takes more energy than Wise Effort. It takes less time for us to call a wise friend or mentor, search out a meeting, reflect in our journal, or meditate than it does to search out mind altering substances. And that doesn't include the time required to rectify the mess we make when we relapse.

But Wise Effort does take energy. It is not something that we can just lull ourselves into. I do not consider myself to have a strong meditative practice. Therefore, I go to a meditation class on Saturday morning. It only meets once a week, but the energy I extend to going to class helps me concentrate on meditation throughout the week. Even though my practice is weak, I have sometimes had the opportunity to lead the class and have been complimented on the quality instruction I provided. We seek continuous improvement, not immediate perfection.

I know that an excellent way for me to begin my day is by chanting "The Homage to the Buddha," "The Three Refuges," and "The Five Precepts." It takes only two minutes of effort. Yet too often I am driving to campus or putzing around my house when I realize that I didn't take those two minutes. Yet, my Wise Intention helps keep the precepts in my mind throughout the day even when I don't follow through with Wise Action. This is not ideal, but it is not a failure either.

Too many times, we put our effort into recounting those areas where we have not done our best or have not lived up to our expectations of ourselves. Had the person I knew decided to focus on their poor choice—which they will need to reflect on eventually—they might not have had the effort to maintain their sobriety.

Elements in *Wise Effort*

The background is a detail from a photograph of Nicola Tesla reading a book in his Colorado Springs laboratory (1900). Tesla does not appear in this image. The peasant hoeing his carrots was published in Ibn Butlan of Baghdad's *Tacuinum Sanitatis* (15th century). Five versions of Taki Katei's *Lotus in Bloom* (19th century) are on the bottom. The *Octopus vulgaris* is a watercolor created by Kawahara Keiga (c. 1823 – 1829). An image of the emaciated Buddha completes this piece.

Wise Mindfulness

My Buddhist practice is very simple. I am more apt to read Thich Nhat Hanh's *Breath, You Are Alive!* or Pema Chodron's *Comfortable with Uncertainty* than I am to read the *suttas* themselves or formal commentary on them. But very soon after I started to live my life based on the Buddha *dhamma*, I read and studied the *Satipaṭṭhāna Sutta* and Analayo's book length analysis *Satipatthana: The Direct Path to Realization*.

I am not sure exactly why I picked up this *sutta* and spent so much time one Summer reading it over and over while also studying various commentaries about it. Maybe it was because I was told that it was one of the most important *suttas* in the Theravada tradition? Maybe I was still being a research geek where Buddhism was still more of an intellectual pursuit than a way of life?

In discussing my simple approach to Buddhism and saying that I prefer the instruction in *The Dhammapada* to reading the collections of long discourses, middle length discourses, and connected discourses—all of which I own in translation—I am not suggesting that studying the *suttas* is anything but valuable. What I am acknowledging is that—for me—it is too easy to focus on intellectual pursuits rather than have an emotional experience.

Bhikkhu Bodi explains that the liberating truth of the *dhamma* can only be realized within oneself. It is not something mysterious or remote. It is not something to be accepted merely on faith or be believed in based on the authority of books or teachers. He writes that "In the practice of right mindfulness, the mind is trained to remain in the present, open, quiet, and alert contemplating the present event."

As an academic who does research on *karuna* (compassion) as it relates to college teaching, I study Buddhist *suttas* and commentaries as well as other erudite texts. I do believe that my academic learning has had a positive influence on my Buddhist practice. But academic knowledge does not substitute for lived experience. This is especially true for someone who is new to Buddhism and/or recovery.

In my experience, the best way to grow in Wise Mindfulness is not to read about meditation but to practice it. The Gautama Buddha taught four types of meditation: sitting, walking, standing, reclining. Sitting is the most common.

To sit and contemplate on my breath. To feel the short breaths and long breaths. To feel the fullness of my lungs when I inhale. To feel the air on my upper lip as I exhale. To scan my body. To silence my mind. These actions are what bring me into the present when I meditate. These actions allow me to be present while conducting my day to day affairs.

As anyone who meditates knows, Wise Mindfulness takes effort. Even after more than seventeen years of practice, I cannot keep my mind focused for very long. While I am tempted to say that my meditation practice is grossly inadequate, I benefit from even feeble attempts.

Elements in *Wise Mindfulness*

The background is Gustav Klimt's *Garden with Sunflowers* (c. 1912). The head is a lithograph created by N.H. Jacob as an illustration for Dr Bourgery's *Traité complet de l'anatomie de l'homme comprenant la médecine opératoire* (1834). The flower in the mind cavity is a detail of one of Claude Monet's lilies.

The four remaining images represent the four basic postures that a body can assume: walking, standing, sitting, and laying down. Although Samuel Hawks (sitting) and Alexandra David-Neel (walking) are identifiable, these images were not selected because of who they were, rather, what they are doing. Hawks was born c. 1836 as an enslaved person. After he was freed, he moved to Michigan where he became a successful farmer and businessman. During her life, David-Neel was an opera singer, theosophist, Freemason, feminist, anarchist, writer, and Tibetan Buddhist monk. The portrait of the unidentified man (standing) was taken in the nineteenth century. The Buddha (reclining) is the final element.

Wise Concentration

In 1999, Chris Chabris and Dan Simons conducted what is now known as "The Invisible Gorilla Experiment." They showed a video of several people passing a basketball back and forth. Viewers were asked to count the number of times the ball was passed. In the middle of the video, a gorilla walks through the basketball players.

After the video was completed, the researchers asked their viewers how many saw the gorilla. Because they concentrated so hard on the basketball, half of the people watching the basketball players did not see a person dressed as a full sized gorilla walk into the middle of the game, stand for a moment, and then leave the screen.

Usually, we miss the gorilla not because we are concentrating so hard on something else. We miss the gorilla because we are distracted. As I learned while reading Jamie Kreiner's *The Wandering Mind*, modern distractions are not so modern. Christian monks from late antiquity to the medieval period were worried about the distractions of the modern world including those caused by the invention of books. They were worried about how worldly distractions negatively impacted their communities, bodies, memories, and minds. Although they had a very different worldview than I do as a Buddhist, the essence of their concerns are the same concerns addressed in the Buddha *dhamma*.

One way to practice Wise Concentration is to meditate on an object for a sustained period of time. Eventually, the meditator will experience rapture by finding joy in their interest of the object.

Happiness is felt by the person meditating when they successfully concentrate. One-pointedness is the final factor of such focused meditation and happens when the object and mind become unified.

Because I have rarely been able to concentrate for such an extended period, I find the process of momentary concentration to be more useful. In this form of concentration, the person meditating does not try to fixate on an individual object in exclusion of other objects. Instead, they allow for continuous awareness of what is going on in the mind.

When I go to temple, I turn off my phone so that I can better concentrate. I take the same approach to other areas of my life. For example, when I tried to grade assignments or to concentrate on various tasks, I was often distracted by email notifications that popped up on my screen. I now turn off email when I want to concentrate on other tasks.

Because I live alone, I have a great deal of control over the distractions in my environment, except at 7:00am and 6:30pm when it is time to serve Pichi, my dog, her breakfast and dinner. Friends know that they can text me 24 hours a day. But they also know that I have my phone off when I am working. I do not attend recovery meetings online, but, if I did, I would shut off all other windows and turn off my phone so that I would not face distractions. I can choose on what I concentrate and, when attending a recovery meeting, my concentration is on sobriety.

My mind still wanders when I meditate. I still miss gorillas that cross my path. But I know that if I continue to follow the Noble Eightfold Path that my concentration will continue to improve. Someday, I might feel a sense of rapture, happiness, or even one pointedness during meditation. In the meantime, I will be content to concentrate as best I can while working toward improvement.

Elements in *Wise Concentration*

This piece features Henry Ford Justice's illustration of King Kojata for Andrew Lang's *Green Fairy Book* (1892). The social media symbols in the well were designed geralt and released on Pixabay. A wooden Buddha is the final element in this piece.

Appendix: Reflections on Art, Buddhism, and Recovery

Art is not something that should be explained by the artist so that their audience can appreciate the "true" message behind it. Instead, art should begin a dialogue between the piece of art and the viewer. The artist themself has had their say with the creation of the piece of art and now it is time for the viewer of the art to experience their own interactions with it.

The artist might discuss general artistic intent. For example, the pieces in this book are influenced by and are designed to create a reflection on the Buddha *dhamma*. But to try to explicitly explain in any type of detail why each element was selected would only diminish the value of the dialogue between artist and audience. For example, seeing the Four Noble Truths shortly after they were created, someone sent me an excited response that included the question, "Why did you include a Gibson girl in *The Second Noble Truth*?" An accurate answer is "I didn't." But that answer is also inaccurate.

While it is true that no Gibson girl appears in the piece, the piece is designed so that it clearly evokes thoughts of Gibson girls even though I hadn't thought about them until I was asked this question. My friend used his experience to engage with the art.

The question of "Why a Gibson girl?" is worth asking. Reflecting on the non-exist Gibson girl and her inclusion in the piece and how she and the art relate to the Second Noble Truth provides richer insight than if the viewer were left only with my explanation.

I love hearing people's reactions to my art because they allow me to have a richer insight into what I have created and why it matters. It also allows me to ponder connections that I had not directly intended but which are clearly present, at least to that individual viewer.

My reflections on the art are clearly not explanations of the art. Writing them allowed me to share some of my thoughts on how art, sobriety, and the Buddha *dhamma* intersect in my life.

There are some aspects of my art that I don't mind talking about. For example, the octopuses that appear in several places reference the Noble Eightfold Path. But why include them where I did? I look to you for an explanation.

Another choice I made that I am willing to discuss is my habit of using older photographs and pieces of art, specifically from 1927 or earlier. There is a practical reason for this choice: copyright law. In 2023, the year I was creating the art, something published during 1927 or earlier is automatically in the public domain. I can legally use it without seeking permission or having to build a case for fair use. Those practical considerations have led to an artistic voice that I cherish. If copyright law suddenly changed and I could legally incorporate any image I wanted into my art, I still think I would favor older pieces.

With two exceptions, the post 1927 elements are either no longer covered under copyright law for various reasons or were released under a Creative Commons or some other license that allows for their legal use. I am indebted to Pixabay for being such a wonderful source of such images. For what two elements am I prepared to mount a fair use defense if I were sued? I'm not foolish enough to draw attention to them. I am only foolish enough to say that they exist somewhere in this book.

I hope that the art provokes thoughtful responses from you. And if my reflections assist your own reflecting, I am grateful. But, ultimately, *Addiction Recovery Through Buddhist Wisdom* is your book and I hope that you create your own art throughout its pages.

Elements in *Reflections on Art, Recovery, and Buddhism*

This piece combines a Bhutanese thanka from Mt. Meru and the Buddhist University (19th century) and a photograph of John Singer Sargent painting at Fladbury (c. 1888-89).

Made in the USA
Monee, IL
21 September 2023